THE OFFICIAL
LAWYER'S
HANDBOOK

(How to Survive a Legal Career)

by

DANIEL R. WHITE

and

PHILIP R. JENKS

A HARRIMAN HOUSE BOOK

HARRIMAN HOUSE PUBLISHING

'THE OFFICIAL LAWYER'S HANDBOOK' by Daniel R. White :
Copyright © Daniel R. White 1991. Published by arrangement with New
American Library, a division of Penguin Books USA Inc.

Pages 154-155 are reproduced by permission of Times Newspapers Ltd,
and first appeared in The Times on 6th February 1992.

First print: September 1992
Reprinted: December 1992
Reprinted: September 1993
Reprinted: January 1995

British Library Cataloguing-in-Publication Data

A CIP record for this book is available from the British Library.

ISBN 1-897597-00-2

Printed and bound in Great Britain by
Holbrooks Printers Ltd
Norway Rd
Hilsea
Portsmouth
Hants
PO3 5HX

CONTENTS

Q: What makes a lawyer laugh ?

A : Humour from the Bench

"A shell to thee, and a shell to thee,
but the oyster is the lawyer's fee."

DANIEL R. WHITE practised corporate law and litigation for several years in Washington, D.C., before devoting all his time to writing and lecturing.

PHILIP JENKS qualified as a solicitor with a London firm before starting HARRIMAN HOUSE.

INTRODUCTION

Three years ago, when the OLH first came out, the UK economy was in deep guano. Property values had crashed, companies were going bust at record rates, and the fantastic era of mergers and acquisitions was but a fond memory. Whole departments in big law firms had nothing to do except contemplate their impending doom.

The only safe area to be in was insolvency. As business after business went down the tubes, the lawyers who specialised in corporate euthanasia never had it so good. They spent long profitable hours firing bullets of mercy into the heads of expiring conglomerates, over-geared property companies and beleaguered parts of the Maxwell legacy. Dirty work indeed, but then life is dirty – ask the guys who clear up after the Charrington Clydesdales.

So how, in the mid-Nineties, does the legal profession find itself, and what does the future hold?

The lesson to be learned from the last six years is that lawyers are not insulated from the rest of the economy nor from the pain which a downturn brings. In 1986 City partnerships talked excitedly of growth, bonuses and foreign offices. Less than a year later the same partners muttered darkly about downsizing, budgets and "if we don't get rid of twenty bodies by

Christmas, I'll be earning less than twice what some of my clients earn." The downturn was sudden and it was savage.

The upturn, to the extent that it exists, has been sparked by a modest pick-up in corporate activity together with growth in one or two specific areas: environment, energy, and media work, for instance. But the general picture is still far from rosy. The profession as a whole is hurting bad. Consider:

Blood-Letting

In the recession firms got into the habit of firing staff. They had to. Now, though things are slightly better, the risk of being 'let go' still hangs over every lawyer who doesn't have a gilt-edged client following. At one City firm assistants told to take a walk used to be given a six-month grace period to find another job. Now that grace period is four weeks and the word on the street is that it's coming down to an hour and a half.

This blood-letting owes much to the American axiom – 'Lose your worst lawyers this year or you'll lose your best ones next year'. Senior Partners are cutting away the deadwood because they fear that junior partners and senior assistants, the people who really make the money, will go elsewhere.

There is no safety now even for partners, traditionally as exempt from quality and productive requirements as the Royal Family. Unproductive partners are being eased out or forcibly dumped as if they were mere assistants. And because of what? *Dispensability* – which in preceding decades was virtually a badge of honour for a lawyer, the quintessence of achievement.

Some take comfort from the fact that the only people getting the boot are those whose firms were already looking for an excuse to get rid of them – in effect, freeriders. Maybe, but consider the implications: If you weed out the slowest five runners in a ten person race, the average pace goes up for everyone. Law firms are speeding up, going faster and harder than ever, and it's going to be that way for some time to come.

Quality Work

In the 80s, lawyers were apt to boast about the 'quality work' they were doing. What elevated mere 'work' to *'quality* work' was its fee-generating potential and the perceived glamour of the task (or more usually the client) and had nothing to do with intellectual reward. *Ergo,* corporate work was quality; private client work wasn't.

Lawyers don't talk so much about quality work nowadays; it's enough to be doing any work at all, quality or not. Weaned fat on corporate wheeling and dealing in the 1980s they now suck gratefully on any dry old tit that dangles within reach.

Fees

The downturn in work has put the squeeze on fees and no mistakin'. Cost-conscious clients have taken advantage of a buyers' market and made it known that they will shop around for the best deal. In-house lawyers, traditionally looked down upon as lawyers who couldn't cut the mustard in private practice (only in *some* cases unfairly), carry the whip hand. They know it, the firms know it, and fees reflect it.

Beauty parades for big work are standard. Negotiation over fees is tolerated, if not exactly welcomed. Clients are, possibly for the first time ever, being treated like clients. Some firms, like Davies Arnold Cooper, provide their clients with estimates of fees and costs at any stage of a case. Fixed fees for specified jobs are not uknown. And some of the larger firms have, without question, been buying in work at prices which yield no profit at all but which at least pay the rent and cover the salaries. In 1992-93 this cut-price work kept whole teams of highly experienced lawyers ungainfully and miserably employed.

What we are witnessing is a re-distribution of power in the client/professional relationship. Just as NHS reforms have forced snooty consultants to speak to common or garden (but *fundholding*) GPs, so recession has been a great leveller in the legal market.

Salaries

In 1991-92 assistant salaries did the unthinkable: after a decade of regular sizeable increases they actually went down. Not by much. Only a few per cent, but it seems like a lot

Eighteen Good Reasons to Become a Lawyer

➤ The money.

➤ You think people who carry oversized black briefcases have an aura of worldly power.

➤ The money.

➤ You're a genius, you know it, and you think becoming a lawyer is the best way to make sure everyone else knows it.

➤ You want to change the world.

➤ You want to own the world.

➤ You're going thin on top and you think wearing a wig at the Bar is the most sophisticated way to conceal your gleaming solar panel.

➤ You want to get out of doing jury service.

➤ The money.

➤ When you were twelve, you spent your entire savings on a train set that broke down in two hours, since when your sole aim in life has been to sue the swine who sold it to you and reduce him to servile beggary.

➤ The money.

➤ You were President of your University debating team and always loved the look on the face of your opponent as you ripped his argument to pieces.

➤ You think most male lawyers look like Harry Hamlin.

➤ You think most female lawyers look like Glenn Close

➤ You're Jewish and don't want to be a doctor.

➤ You want to teach law because it's common knowledge that law tutors have lots of affairs with their students.

➤ The money.

➤ Why not? Everyone else is.

when your salary is the one thing that makes it worthwhile getting out of bed in the morning.

From that low ebb, things have improved a little. For the first time in four years, salaries are going up. Those qualified for between two and four years are most in demand and are seeing their salaries rise by 3% to 5% annually. The major City firms are maintaining their fixed salary bands but probably only because they know that there are plenty of niche West End and provincial firms trying to cherry-pick their talent.

At the height of the recession, the one sector of the law bucking the trend was insolvency. Experienced insolvency lawyers could almost name their price. The good news for the economy is that insolvency lawyers are no longer quite so flavoursome. The bones of corporate Britain have been picked clean.

The High Street solicitor, meanwhile, is on the ropes. The recession brought the housing market to a standstill, removing a vital source of fee income, and what conveyancing work remains is subject to intense price competition.

Public Image

If the money's a bit tighter and the competition a lot hotter, at least being a lawyer still carries kudos, right?

Wrong.

The profession's image is cracking under the strain of well-publicised fraud within its ranks, and general dissatisfaction with the judicial process. From multiple mortgage frauds, to defrauding the legal aid Green Form scheme, to simple raids on the client account for cash, the profession's readiness to break the law has never been more open to view. In 1994, two hundred and thirty solicitors were charged with misconduct by the Solicitors Disciplinary Tribunal. The Law Society's compensation scheme for victims of professional fraud paid out a whopping £30 million, a sum to which every solicitor had to contribute £1,000.

Lawyer-bashing has not yet become a national sport, as it has in the US. It is still marginally more prestigious to be a lawyer than a griddle-minder at McDonalds. The truly frightening prospect for many trainee lawyers is that, on passing Finals, a McJob may well be the best offer on the table. (see below)

New Bugs

Nearly one in three of the students who pass their solicitor's exams this year will not go on to qualify because of a shortage of training places in law firms. Clients are suffering, which means law firms are suffering – and the demand for new trainees who know fresh air about anything useful has plummeted. The Law Society predicts that there will only be 4,400 places in 1995/96 for the 6,500 students on the Legal Practice Course.

It's worth considering, if you read this book as a prospective trainee, whether you really want to be one of a flood of eager beavers graduating into a profession with no vacancies.

So . . a kinder, gentler profession in the nineties?

Hardly.

"Let me get this straight. The perpetrator, a blond Caucasian female, trespassed on your land, broke into your dwelling, consumed perishable foodstuffs, and slept in your beds. Is that right?"

A thousand points of light?

More like a thousand pints of blood.

So what? For most people, news about starving lawyers carries its own justification. It's inherently pleasing.

But if you're a lawyer yourself, in the process of becoming one, or even just thinking about it, the 'so what' is that the competition in the legal profession is more vicious than ever. You need all the help you can get.

You need this book!

The OLH walks you through every step of your career, from pre-exam bowel-liquification to partnership. Starting with that make-or-break first year of your law degree, it provides enough key concepts and buzzwords to put you at the top of your class – as well as into bed with at least two of your fellow undergraduates by the Christmas holidays.

But this book is more than just a ticket to success in university and law school. It's an *alternative* to both of them, offering better preparation for a legal career than anything you'll get at the College of Law or Inns of Court. It offers not only obscure jargon and archaic concepts, but sufficient training in the art of hair-splitting and issue-obfuscation to enable you to alienate complete strangers in the space of just minutes – a skill that some lawyers don't acquire for weeks. All this for under a tenner!

If you're already out of law school,

Fourteen Hard Facts about Lawyers
(Do you realise what they actually *do* for a living?)

➢ The *average* lawyer earns less per hour than a bus driver (although they get about the same amount of exercise)

➢ The odds are three-to-one that you personally will not do as well as the average lawyer (See Hard Fact No.1)

➢ Everyone you know despises lawyers.

➢ The thought of spending eighty per cent of the rest of your waking life behind a desk makes you want to throw up.

➢ Recent research has shown that seventy-eight per cent of practising lawyers are wider at the stomach than the shoulders.

➢ People charged with murder and rape – your likely clients if you practise criminal law – are usually guilty as sin.

➢ The number of law graduates who get jobs at the top-earning firms is about the same as the number who become jackaroos on Australian sheep farms, and the latter are happier.

➢ Saddam Hussein used to be thought of as a nice guy before he attended law school.

➢ A 'light day' in a large law firm runs from 8 a.m. to 8 p.m.

➢ A 'light' week consists of six and a half light days.

➢ Harry Hamlin gets more sex in one episode of L.A. Law than five hundred real lawyers get in a year.

➢ Most male lawyers look more like John Mortimer than Harry Hamlin.

➢ So do most female lawyers.

➢ Studies show that the average law tutor has only 7.3 sexual encounters with law students per year.

the OLH is even more critical. It shows you how to get into one of those prestigious high-paying law firms and, more difficult, how to survive once you're there.

You didn't go to law school so you could spend the next five years selling life insurance to your friends. You've already done all that. They're not your friends any more. You're ready now for the status that comes from doing something truly useless. You're ready now to be a . . a . .

LAWYER

And not just any kind of lawyer. Not for you a two-room office above Rumbelows in Peckham High Street. You want to be a legal honcho – an adviser to politicians, privatised utility bosses, and other big-time swindlers. You want a plush office, embossed stationery, a calfskin briefcase, and a secretary who has the organisational skills of a Cray mainframe. But with nicer legs. The OLH tells you how to get them.

It's not just for lawyers, though. It's also essential reading for "lay people" (what lawyers call the people they screw).

Who has not at one time or another said "I'm going to sue the bastard if it's the last thing I do!" The rub is, only a lawyer knows *how* to sue the bastard. If you, a lay person, want to start an action, you have to instruct a lawyer which, like hiring a member of an even older profession, may be easy but it's not cheap.

The legal profession is too important to remain veiled in secrecy. It pervades our existence. Whether you want to start a business, buy a house, or sue the doctor who assured you that the sex change operation was reversible, you need to know the law. To your utter distaste, you'll have to deal with a lawyer.

But you don't have to be at your lawyer's mercy simply because up to now you've never understood what he was up to.

Read this book, and you'll know where your lawyer is coming from, how he got there, and just where 'there' is. You'll know what lawyers do – and how to stop them from doing it to you.

CHAPTER ONE

DETERMINING YOUR LEGAL APTITUDE

'Tunnel-visioned workaholic
.. or double-visioned alcoholic?'

Not everyone is cut out for a legal career. Before beginning the training in this book, take the following self-assessment test to find out whether you have what it takes to be a lawyer, or whether you would be more usefully employed in a productive sector of the economy. You might discover that you really aren't suited to it at all. Better to find out now, before your vocabulary becomes permanently encrusted with Latin.

You might also discover, if your score is high, that you aren't suited to anything *but* the law – in which case this book will prove to have been the best investment of your life.

1. **When you wake up each day, the first thing you do is:**

    (a) Hit the snooze control.

    (b) Turn on the afternoon news to see what you missed that morning.

    (c) Try to ascertain the age, gender, and species of whatever is sleeping beside you, without waking it up.

    (d) Make the bed, polish your shoes, write a letter to mother, and recite the White Book – all before breakfast.

2. **If a partner told you to spend the next two weeks proofreading the Encyclopaedia Britannica, you would:**

   (a) Lose your lunch on the spot.

   (b) Say that as flattered as you are to receive such an important job, Farr told you only yesterday that he dreams of that sort of work, and you'd be willing to stand aside for him just this once.

   (c) Reply that you don't see any reason why you couldn't complete the job by next Monday.

   (d) Grimace but resign yourself to the task.

3. **When you were a child, you experienced lust in the presence of:**

   (a) Your parent of the opposite sex.

   (b) Your parent of the same sex.

   (c) Either parent's briefcase.

   (d) Your Great Dane, Chewy.

4. *Word Association.* **When you hear the word** *prison,* **the thing that comes to mind is:**

   (a) Violent criminals.

   (b) Your last income tax return.

   (c) Your boarding school.

   (d) Unsafe sex.

5. **At the end of** *Dances with Wolves* **you were left with:**

   (a) A feeling of emptiness at the destruction of the Sioux tribe.

   (b) A feeling of emptiness after watching a three hour film on a packet of popcorn.

   (c) A new-found appetite for pacy Bruce Willis thrillers.

   (d) A new-found appetite for raw buffalo heart.

6. **Your favourite colour is:**

   (a) Caribbean blue.

   (b) Conference-table brown.

   (c) Green – broken up by pictures of former Lord Chancellors.

   (d) Yellow – preferably 8" by 11" with narrow margins.

7. *Word Association.* **When you hear the word** *security,* **the first thing that comes to mind is:**

(a) The blanket you keep under your pillow.

(b) The 72-function Swiss Army knife you carry in your pocket whenever you visit friends South of the river.

(c) Negligence insurance.

(d) A comfort letter from Linklaters & Paines.

8. **If you were to run over a dog that had darted into the street, your first impulse would be to:**

(a) Feel concern that it might be alive and suffering.

(b) Try to find the owner to say how sorry you are.

(c) Try to find the owner to demand payment for the dent in your car.

(d) Reverse over it again to teach it a lesson.

9. **When you think of lawyers, you envision people who:**

(a) Protect the downtrodden.

(b) Exploit the proletariat.

(c) Couldn't get job in productive sectors of the economy.

(d) You try not to think about lawyers.

10. **Which of the following do you consider most likely to guarantee success in the law?**

(a) A precise, analytical mind.

(b) The ability to lie like a politician.

(c) A-level Latin

(d) This book.

11. **If a sexual opportunity presented itself right now, you would:**

(a) Go for it, no matter where you are, who you're with, or what it might do to the rest of your life.

(b) Ascertain whether he/she has some form of contraception, has anything that looks like a cold sore, or shows more than a passing interest in the plot of *Basic Instinct.*

(c) Call all your friends to let them know it's finally about to happen.

(d) Be too stunned to act.

12. **During your idle moments, you fantasise about:**

(a) Winning a class action against Shell.

(b) Oral arguments before the Court of Appeal.

(c) Oral acts with the models in *Marie Claire*.

(d) Joining a City firm so you wouldn't have to worry about any more idle moments.

13. **The first thing that comes to mind when you look at the ink blot below is:**

(a) The Jackson-Pollock in your firm's conference room

(b) A hit-and-run victim (and potential client).

(c) The insanity defence.

(d) Prefer to research the issue before commenting.

14. **Your idea of a great time is:**

(a) A late night at the office proofreading Loan Agreements.

(b) Around-the-clock negotiations on a corporate takeover.

(c) Foreclosing a mortgage on a widow with six young handicapped children.

(d) Nothing remotely resembling any of the above.

NOW CHECK YOUR SCORE

POINTS TALLY

1. (a) 0 (b) 1 (c) 2 (d) 7
2. (a) 0 (b) 1 (c) 7 (d) 2
3. (a) 1 (b) 1 (c) 6 (d) 2
4. (a) 5 (b) 3 (c) 2 (d) 3
5. (a) 0 (b) 4 (c) 5 (d) 6
6. (a) 0 (b) 4 (c) 4 (d) 7
7. (a) 0 (b) 2 (c) 2 (d) 7

8. (a) 0 (b) 0 (c) 5 (d) 7
9. (a) 2 (b) 5 (c) 0 (d) 0
10. (a) 0 (b) 5 (c) 4 (d) 7
11. (a) 1 (b) 5 (c) 3 (d) 1
12. (a) 5 (b) 7 (c) 1 (d) 7
13. (a) 1 (b) 5 (c) 5 (d) 7
14. (a) 7 (b) 6 (c) 7 (d) 0

EVALUATION

65 - 93 points

Congratulations – sort of. You are compulsive, calculating, avaricious, sexually repressed, and no doubt already too blind to go out without a dog. You could make it to the very top of the legal profession.

45 - 64 points

Not bad. You have the makings of a lawyer, maybe even partnership material. Sometimes you let your feelings for humanity interfere with your professional role, but with work you could learn to repress those feelings.

20 - 44 points

Okay, so you're not going to be the youngest partner in your firm's history. So what? You're a likeable person with a bright life ahead of you. Enjoy!

0 - 20 points

You've gone too far the other way. You're a weak-kneed hand-wringing jellyfish without an ounce of gumption. Pull yourself together and try to make something of your life – but not in the law.

CHAPTER TWO

GETTING ONTO A LAW DEGREE COURSE

'Square Pegs in Square Holes'

University law departments aren't interested in the 'whole person' or in developing individuality. Quite the reverse: their objective is to pick applicants of uniform squareness, and over the next three years to hone, sand and polish them until they match each other as perfectly as a pair of Bentley Mulsanne clutch plates.

So you swam the Channel in ski boots, and you play the harp? Big deal! You run your parish Wine Society, and were the first male in your school's history to play Lady Macbeth. So what? You yodel for Kent and have a bitch that was placed at Crufts. Bully for you! Law departments need wacky individuals like the *Titanic* needed on-board ice trays.

Law departments look at one thing and one thing only: exam results. They just plug the figures into a formula and accept as many applicants as they have room for, discounted by the number of people who will die, go to other schools, or decide there must be a less painful way to gird one's loins for life.

What about those application forms requiring numerous referees to testify to your terrific character? Don't they suggest that some sort of selection process is going on?

They do. But they represent ways of *weeding people out*, not bringing them in. Your application might show you to be barely literate, notwithstanding the distinction you got for your A-level business studies project "Best Begging Pitches on the London Underground." Your references might say only that your methadone treatment appears to be working.

The good news is that there are loads of places to go round. There are more than seventy universities and colleges offering law degrees which give exemption from the CPE, and over seven thousand places available.

*"Before he went to law school, he either agreed or disagreed
with my opinions. Now he concurs or dissents."*

Any literate primate can get in *somewhere*.

But it's getting tougher. One of the consequences of the downturn in financial markets is that today's young-and-greedy are returning to the law in droves. Programmes like *LA Law* have given the profession a kind of highbrow chic, which is ironic, as they depict legal practice about as accurately as the pages of *Hello* depict marital bliss.

The bad news is that the job prospects the other end are looking distinctly dicy. That's why it's so important to get into a college that the law firms have heard of (and remember you'll be interviewing for your traineeship in your final year). The only sure way of doing that is to go like hell for those exam results. There may be some well-rounded likeable people in the top firms, but that isn't what got them there. Straight A grades are the sort of thing you should be aiming for.

So . . . have you got what it takes to make it in the law? Is your mind a steel trap or a lump of tofu?

The test on the opposite page has been devised to help you find out.

READING COMPREHENSION

1. *"It was the best of times, it was the worst of times, it was the age of wisdom, it was the age of foolishness .... it is a far far better rest that I go to than I have ever known."*

Question: In the above novel, what time is it?

(a) The best of times

(b) The worst of times

(c) The Sunday Times

(d) About two o'clock

2. *"Know thyself."*

Question: In the above passage, the writer is:

(a) Plagiarizing Plato.

(b) Employing an archaic usage.

(c) Advocating a solipsistic approach to epistemology.

(d) Describing your social life.

ANALYTICAL REASONING

1. Einstein's theory of relativity postulated that there can be no motion at a speed greater than that of light in a vacuum, and time is dependent on the relative motion of an observer measuring the time. If a hydrogen atom electron is accelerated at a rate of π / speed of light through an inverse hypermagnetic positron field and and then bombarded with neutrons from a nuclear hemorrhopidal pile in a critical core reaction, what time is it?

(a) The best of times.

(b) The worst of times.

(c) Time to think about business school.

(d) About two o'clock.

2. *For a dinner party, Sophie must prepare several different three-bean salads, using chilli beans, lentil beans, lima beans, kidney beans, soya beans, and garbanzos. Unfortunately: (i) lima beans and lentils do not taste good together; (ii) kidney beans and soya beans do not look good together; (iii) chilli beans and garbanzos will render her guests incapable of holding solid food.* Within these restrictions, write down the combinations of bean which fulfil the following descriptions:

(a) Seven salads that resemble the bottom of a bird cage.

(b) Four that will have her guests exchanging glances within a few mouthfuls.

(c) Three that her pet goat would not eat.

(d) None of the above. If you want to count beans, take your accountancy exams.

3. Ramona said *"All dogs bark. This animal does not bark. Therefore this animal is not a dog."* Which of the following most closely parallels the logic of the above syllogism?

(a) Cats do not bark. Cats climb trees. Trees have bark.

(b) Lawyers overcharge. Taxi meters overcharge. Lawyers are taxi meters.

(c) Fred sells cars. Every car sold by Fred falls apart. Fred is a Fiat dealer.

(d) Dogs bay at the moon. Your girlfriends bay at the moon. You would be better off getting to know thyself.

EVALUATION OF FACTS

1. Murder consists of (i) the death of a human being, and (ii) an intent to cause death or g.b.h. Apply these rules to the following factual situation:

Ronnie, a Manchester scrap metal dealer, enters Jean-Paul's Unisex Barber-shop in a tough section of town. While he is waiting for a trim, an employee of Jean-Paul's sees him and, mistaking him for somebody else, runs a chain saw through the upper half of his head.

Question: On trial for murder, the employee should be found:

(a) Guilty of taking too much off the top.

(b) Not guilty because of assumption-of-risk principles regarding unisex hairdressers.

(c) Guilty, but nevertheless qualified for the West Midlands Police Force.

(d) About two o'clock.

CHAPTER THREE

PASSING YOUR
LAW DEGREE

*"Are you telling me
Socrates did it this way?"*

Legal lore recognises three distinct periods in the standard three-year degree:

- 1st Year: they *scare* you to death.

- 2nd Year: they *work* you to death.

- 3rd Year: they *bore* you to death.

This is a pretty fair assessment. The most memorable aspect of the first year – fear – follows from having to learn a host of completely alien concepts in such a short time, getting up in time for a 9 o'clock lecture being the one students have most trouble with. It also results from exposure to the Socratic method of teaching, or 'learning through humiliation'. (More on this later.)

This gradually gives way to a period of frenetic overwork brought on by insecurity. Based on the marks each student has been getting in the first few months, only ten per cent of the class now ranks in the top ten per cent of the class – a phenomenon which may have been anticipated by the more reflective of you. But one hundred per cent of the class *is used* to ranking in the top ten per cent.

Those who now make up the bottom ninety per cent feel confused and anxious – even desperate. Consistent with the modus operandi that got them on the course in the first place, they channel these feelings into hard work.

As for the boredom in the third year, you would have noticed this in the first year if you hadn't been so scared.

THE SOCRATIC METHOD

The Socratic method of teaching first became fashionable in the USA and is now gaining in popularity over here. It aims to improve on the typical situation in which a lecturer reads out prepared notes to his students at a nice even pace, and in which they record what he says word for word in their own files. The one problem in this otherwise efficient transfer of knowledge is that it is accomplished without actually troubling anybody's brain.

The Socratic method, by contrast, involves a dialogue between the lecturer and a chosen student, with the student pressed to answer ever more complex levels of questioning on the case or issue under discussion.

It is a controversial teaching method. Its potential pedagogic value indisputably surpasses that of the old-fashioned lecture method, which causes even diligent students to experience bouts of narcolepsy. In practice, however, its shortcomings are severe.

Firstly, very few tutors are willing to jettison all those lecture notes they took so many years to compile, and even fewer are capable of replacing their notes with effective Socratic teaching. Innumerable class hours are wasted in the following way:

TUTOR SMITH: Ms Ellis, are you with us today?

STUDENT ELLIS : Yes.

TUTOR SMITH: Then let us proceed. What am I thinking?

STUDENT ELLIS: I beg your pardon?

TUTOR SMITH: What thought is passing through my mind at this moment?

STUDENT ELLIS: Uh . . .I don't know . . .it could be . . . I'm not quite . . .

TUTOR SMITH: Ms Ellis, did you have a look at the case we talked about in yesterday's session?

STUDENT ELLIS: Yes! I read it – twice in fact. It was about Section 14(b) of the Race Relations Act.

TUTOR SMITH: If you've read it, *as you claim*, why are you unable to answer a simple question regarding the RRA?

The other practical problem with the Socratic Method is that tutors who are either lazy or uninterested in teaching use it to kill time and avoid having to prepare a lecture:

TUTOR RYAN: Mr Lane, how did you get on with the cases on this week's reading list?

STUDENT LANE: They were fine. Are you thinking of any one in particular?

TUTOR RYAN: Pick any one you want and tell us whether you agreed or disagreed with the judgement?

STUDENT LANE: Well, I remember one that I thought made sense.

TUTOR RYAN: Good. Now, let's see .. Ms Henson, do you agree or disagree with the case Mr Lane is referring to?

STUDENT HENSON: I'm not sure which one he *is* referring to.

TUTOR RYAN: Mr Lane, please elucidate the case to which you are referring to Ms Henson.

This sort of thing is a far cry from the teaching system that produced Plato. If Socrates was alive today, he'd be turning in his grave.

NOTE: Just because a tutor calls out your name doesn't mean you have to answer. If he doesn't know you personally (most won't), just keep quiet and pretend you're not there – the 'foxhole' technique. The only problem is that students who do know you may give the game away by looking in your direction. If this happens, turn and stare intently at the person sitting beside you.

> University Law departments have been described as a place for the accumulation of learning: First-year students bring some in; third-year students take none away. Hence it accumulates.

LAW STUDENTS AND LAW TUTORS

As a law student you will have to learn to deal with two sets of people: other students and tutors. The former have to be dealt with because they're physically ubiquitous – in the classroom, at the campus cafeteria, on that library sofa where you were hoping to take a nap. The latter have to be dealt with because they're *psychologically* omnipresent, hovering about like superegos that speak in Latin.

Other Students

Although your fellow students will come in all sizes, colours, pedigrees, and genders, they will fall into a few easily identifiable categories:

The Mainstreamer

Most of your classmates will have come straight from school to university and will be planning to go straight from university to law school. Some will have chosen their career out of driving ambition. Others will have been forced into it by their parents. Most will have done it because they couldn't think of anything else to do.

If male, the Mainstreamer's dress is conventional, his hair is short, his politics moderate to conservative, and his personal habits unremarkable. If female, her dress is conventional, her politics mildly feminist, and her willingness to have sex dependent on whether the relationship is 'meaningful'.

By and large, you will be able to understand and enjoy these people. You are probably one of them.

The Keenie

Keenies are the most conspicuous as well as the most objectionable feature of university law departments. They have their hands in the air throughout lectures, pleading for an opportunity to discuss arcane points of law which they have discovered in *unrequired* reading. At the end of each class, they will bolt from their seats (invariably front and centre) to the podium, where they will trap the lecturer and further attempt to display their mastery of the obscure.

The psychology of the Keenie is pitiable. Deeply anxious and insecure, she degrades herself regularly by brown-nosing authority figures – not just lecturers and tutors, but law librarians, security guards and checkout crones in the campus cafeteria.

The important fact to remember is that the Keenie's embarrassing behaviour reflects her internal problems, *not* the realities of passing a law degree. The Keenie is no more likely to get a 2:1 than you are.

You cannot always ignore the Keenie. Her excesses force their way into your life. But you should resist the temptation to solder a steel muzzle to her face.

Lecturers know how to deal with Keenies because every yearly intake has them. Keenies are as old as the law itself.

The Reformer

A number of your classmates will be mature students who have taken up law out of pure economic

The Keenie

LAW SCHOOL BINGO

This pastime is one of the most entertaining aspects of any law degree. The more Keenies you have in your lecture hall the better. Before the lecture, someone distributes cards with the names of the most obnoxious Keenies laid out in a grid, like numbers on a Bingo card. Each card is slightly different. As given Keenies put their arms in the air to ask questions and are called upon by the lecturer, you cross their names off your card. The first person to cross out all the names on his card shouts "Bingo!" and has won.

(A word to the wise: if yours is ever the waving hand whose recognition by the lecturer triggers a shout of "Bingo!" followed by titters and perhaps a few murmurs of disappointment, give some serious thought to whether your classroom conduct would benefit from a touch of restraint.)

necessity. Often they'll already have experience in social work, counselling, local government or some other field not renowned for its wealth-creating potential. They've switched to law because they think it will allow them to promote social reform *and* afford more than one Pot Noodle a day.

The Reformer has a hint of pathos about her, because she sees all too clearly that what could have been the next generation of philosophers, historians and scientists is being transmogrified into an army of litigators, corporate proofreaders and tax gurus.

Don't feel too sorry for her. She may be disillusioned and subversive, but she represents strong competition.

The Computerhead

The primary distinguishing feature of the Computerhead is that he did 'A' levels in physics, chemistry or some other 'hard' science.

You can recognise him by his bottle-bottom glasses and his ability to wear a brown zipped cardigan and grey Hush Puppies without a trace of self-consciousness

The Computerhead has a habit of hanging round the campus computer centre on Saturday nights to meet women. He does this for three years even though he never meets any.

Law Tutors

Law tutors are a proudly idiosyncratic lot. Being as weird as you want is a major perk of academia, and some law professors wouldn't look out of place in the Munster Family. Neverthless, like their students, law tutors fall into identifiable categories.

The Recognised Authority

Most law departments have at least one tutor recognised as an authority on his subject – So and so on Company Law, thingummy on Evidence, whatsisface on Brain Death. (The main difference between brain death and ordinary death, by the way, is that with the latter you're not guaranteed a job with British Rail).

There is only a chance correlation, if any, between status as a Recognised Authority and teaching ability. The Recognised Authority didn't attain that status by devoting lots of time to teaching. His lectures consist of 'Cases I advised on' and 'Lords of Appeal I call by their first names'.

Some Recognised Authorities with expertise in tax and other commercial areas, maintain lucrative consulting contracts with big City firms in the 'one-day-per-week' to which their teaching contracts purport to restrict such activities.

Recognised Authorities in less commercial areas such as civil procedure manage to convert their expertise into hard cash by publishing £35.00 casebooks that their classes are required to buy.

The Fuzzhead

Fuzzhead law tutors specialise in areas of breathtaking obscurity. They know absolutely everything there is to know about Road Traffic Law in Norman England, the Laws of Burial, Cremation and Exhumation, or some other area no one else wants to touch.

The Fuzzhead may be brilliant, but the same escapist impulses that got him into his area of expertise render him unable to relate to other warm-blooded bipeds. He is a consistently miserable teacher, particularly when required to teach mainstream courses such as Contracts or Evidence. He should be avoided unless he has known propensities to mark generously – or unless you are of the Fuzzhead ilk yourself.

The Old Curmudgeon

The Old Curmudgeon is a classic feature of law departments. Sometimes a former Recognised Authority grown irrascible in his twilight years, he is dogmatic, demanding, impatient, crotchety, and surly – on a good day.

The Old Curmudgeon conducts his classes like a Regimental Sergeant-Major: you *will* attend all of his classes; you *will* be in your seat when he arrives; you *will* be prepared to discuss any case on the reading list.

The only way to deal with the Old Curmudgeon is craven capitulation. If he accuses you of poor preparation, shamefully apologise. If he charges you with genetic idiocy, lament your forebears' tradition of inbreeding.

Take comfort in the knowledge that the humiliation you risk by entering his class every day is no greater than that risked by your classmates. Take additional comfort in the knowledge that the Old Curmudgeon may not last another term.

The Young Star

Law departments are forever in search of the Young Star, someone short on years but long on the right credentials. Early publication of a highly acclaimed treatise, noted for its 'fresh

The Old Curmudgeon

outlook' and 'novel insights' is a sure sign of Young Star status. The fact that the proposals for reform in that treatise have about as much chance of getting off the ground as the European Fighter Aircraft is immaterial.

The Young Star is a colourful figure on the law school campus, with her radical attitude, trendy clothes and preference for mixing with students rather colleagues. Make the most of her refreshing outlook in a singularly dowdy branch of the teaching profession.

The Deadwood

Every law department has a few tutors who don't do anything. Dead-woods don't write articles, don't serve on law reform committees, don't do any private consulting, and don't even prepare their lectures. No one is sure what they do with their time.

Rumour has it that some of them have very nice gardens.

The Entertainer

Many university law lecturers pride themselves on being a bit of a hoot. They like to think they can inject humour into even the most impenetrable legal subject. The fact that they have all the wit and sophistication of Noel's House Party need not concern you. Watching someone failing to be funny is tremendously satisfying.

The problem with the Entertainer is not so much that he wastes time, though many do, but that students are lulled by his levity into thinking he'll be a generous marker, only to get their socks blown off in Finals. Enjoy the Entertainer, but don't slack up in his class any more than in your others. Tape your socks up for his Finals paper.

THE COMMON PROFESSIONAL EXAM IN A NUTSHELL

It's a regrettable fact that if you want to jump aboard the legal gravy train you've got to be standing on Platform 1 when it leaves town. Platform 2.1 will sometimes get you aboard. But the train from Platform 2.2 is the Oblivion Express heading non-stop to Beancounter City.

Another regrettable fact is that law exams, unlike many social science subjects, can't be tackled by writing pages and pages of bullshit. It's impossible to bluff your way through. Most students realise this pretty quickly (some as long as three weeks before Finals) and hit the books like demons. They spend every waking hour trying to ingest, in readily upchuckable form, everything there is to know about certain 'core' subjects*.

Students also study a variety of non-core subjects – rapidly-developing areas like evironmental law, increasingly marginal ones like Canon Law, or the plain non-existent – like International Law. But the core subjects are what your law degree is all about and, what's more, they're all that a practising lawyer needs to know. The following sections set out

*Many students ingest these materials at the same time as they are ingesting their breakfast. Bear in mind that dried Bran Flakes, marmalade and toast crumbs on your textbooks substantially reduce their re-sale value.

all the key concepts and buzzwords in a clearer form than you'll ever get in class.

CONTRACTS

A passing familiarity with the law of contract is all you need to hold yourself out as a commercial lawyer. Leases, loan agreements, trusts, and lots of other documents with highfalutin' names are really just contracts. This should be borne in mind if another lawyer presents you with some document and you have no idea what it is. If it requires signing, and it isn't either a will or something that has to be filed in court, you can call it a contract without fear of being laughed at.

Offer and Acceptance

The entire law of contracts can be summed up in two words: *offer* and *acceptance.*

An offer is what it sounds like:

"Hey, big guy, fifty quid for some action?"

So is an acceptance.

"Sure. But I want the cash up front OK?"

Whether a contract has been formed depends on whether there has been a 'meeting of minds'. The acceptance must match the offer.

Jeremy: *"Type up my thesis, and I'll take you out to lunch."*

Sarah: *"No chance pizza-face."*

In that case, there was no meeting of minds. Sarah's reply did not match Jeremy's offer. No contract was formed.

Both offers and acceptances can be conditional:

Henry: *"I'd love to take you to the Clayderman concert – provided you get rid of that boil on your neck."*

Angela: *"Fair enough. I'll come with you, unless someone else – anyone else – asks me out"*

Consideration

Complicating the law of contracts is the concept of 'consideration'. The law won't enforce any old promise – a promise, for example, to give someone something, as in *"the next time I see you I'm going to give you a knuckle sandwich."* It will only enforce promises given in exchange for some return promise or equivalent sacrifice. The return promise or sacrifice is the consideration which makes the contract enforceable.

No one understands this concept. Why they call it consideration, when it has nothing to do with being nice to someone, is one of the law's well-shrouded mysteries.

Neverthless, at least nominal consideration always has to be there. According to tradition, the delivery of a mere peppercorn would be sufficient consideration for a contract to transfer Canary Wharf complete with a 'Build your own Jubilee Line' kit. (In practice no one in their right mind would blow a whole peppercorn that way.)

That's why even multi-billion pound contracts often start out with the bizarre recital: "For £1.00 and other valuable *consideration*, we the undersigned hereby agree . . ."

At the close of the deal one of the lawyers may actually present the other side with a £1 coin (promptly recording it and billing it to his client with interest.)

Breach

What if a client of yours breaches a contract? What if *you* breach a contract? Should you be embarrassed about it? Should your parents insist that you go through with it?

Not necessarily. Sometimes the law *wants* you to breach a contract. Suppose you've entered a contract to build a house for someone on a piece of land that turns out to have a body of water about the size of, say, the Irish Sea, two feet below the surface. The ground is so soft you couldn't pitch a two-man tent on it, let alone a building.

Do you have to proceed according to the contract, however futile it may be? No. The law doesn't see any point in you getting your feet wet, upsetting yourself, and taking it out on the dog just because of some silly old contract.

All the law requires is that you give the other party enough money to 'make him whole'. In deciding what would 'make him whole' a court would take into account such factors as the cost of building elsewhere, whether either party knew about the water under the land before signing, and the race and class of the parties involved.

Unenforceable Contracts

The law won't enforce certain types of contracts, regardless of the presence of consideration, the absence of breach, or anything else.

One example is a contract which is deemed 'contrary to public policy'. Shylock's pound of flesh bargain would not nowadays be enforced south of the border (some Scottish courts remain very strict) on the grounds that to do so would sanction a quasi-criminal act.

The same is true of contracts made 'under duress'. A court would not require you to perform a contract that you accepted after a man whose last name ended in a vowel made you an offer you couldn't refuse. Of course, few such contracts actually make it to court. And if they do, there's no predicting how a judge will rule after receiving an offer to go swimming in Staines Reservoir in concrete Speedos.

A final category of unenforceable contracts involves 'unconscionable contracts'. Occasionally a judge decides that a given contract is *so* unfair, so grossly one-sided, that there's no way he's going to enforce it. The theory seems to be that no sane and sober person would sign such a contract, and the stronger party must somehow have duped the weaker.

A classic example is the case of the old couple who bought a used Morris Marina (remember that beaut?) from a car dealer in Lewisham. The sale contract carried a disclaimer – in print so small it could only be read with the help of an electron microscope – saying that neither the dealer nor the manufacturer could be held liable for any injuries resulting from defects in the car.

When the steering wheel came off in the wife's hands as she was travelling along the A40 three days later, she ignored the disclaimer and sued.

Despite the disclaimer, the court ruled in her favour, saying the contract was unconscionable. It said that the average consumer has too little bargaining power in relation to big car companies, and the public interest in preventing bodily harm outweighed the presumption that a contract's terms should be enforced.

Liberals hail the judge's decision in that case as a victory for natural justice. Conservatives denounce him as just one more do-gooder venting his sexual frustrations on productive elements of society. The liberals are right. The contract wasn't made between two rational free-acting parties. No sane person would buy a Morris Marina from a used-car dealer in Lewisham.

The preceding case doesn't mean that you as lawyer should get rid of all those unconscionable, illegible disclaimers in your client's Standard Terms of Contract. They serve an important 'dust-in-the-eyes' function, blinding the other party to his actual rights.

Go ahead and include a paragraph saying the purchaser acknowledges having inspected the power-steering system, even though she barely has the know-how to count the tyres. Add a provision to the effect that she supervised the assembly of the car stereo, even though the thing was put together in Taiwan. For good measure, throw in a clause which prevents her from winding the windows up and down more than ten times a year.

The consumer won't even be able to *find* these clauses, much less know they're legally meaningless. When she comes back to complain that the car has all the manoeuvrability of an oil supertanker, that the radio only gets one station, and that it gets a bit stuffy with the windows up at 85 fahrenheit, you can point to these clauses and she'll go away. All you have to worry about is whether you're going to burn in hell for your sins.

PALIMONY – A TRAP FOR THE UN-WEARY

Except in a few special situations, contracts do not need to be in writing to be enforceable. Oral agreements will do. In some instances, contracts need not even be spoken to be enforceable: a court may find an 'implied' contract based on the conduct of the parties.

The most common implied contract relates to co-habitees who split up – and the situation in which one of them sues the other claiming breach of an implied contract of ongoing support. There isn't a lot on the statute book addressing this issue. It's basically a social question, one that turns on the mores of the day. What *are* the legitimate expectations of a woman who accepts an invitation to move in with a man for a couple of years? Is there necessarily a promise of support for life? What if he invites her over for just one evening – has he at least promised to buy her lunch next day?

And what if the tables are turned? She's a rich advertising executive and he's a starving artist who moves into *her* home? Does the whole thing depend on whether they had sexual relations? Should the result be different if he's impotent?

Advising clients in this area is very difficult, partly because the law is unsettled, but mainly because no one wants to take their lawyer along on a date.

For the time being, the best way to ensure safe sex is to supply your lecherous clients of all genders with blank waiver forms (see the sample over the page) which they should have their prospective lovers execute at the first sign of lust, ideally before the first cocktail, and in any event before the Big Bang (a concept that persists in debauchery even if it has been discredited in astronomy.)

PALIMONY WAIVER

1. The Stud [Insert Client's Name]

and

2. The Undersigned Prospective Lover

Period of Relationship Covered by this Waiver: _____
(should not be less than 3 minutes)

The Lover, being of sound mind, nubile body, and substantial libidinous urges, hereby acknowledges the mutual nature of all pleasures and gratifications arising from any carnal relations, consummated or otherwise, between the Lover and the Stud, (said carnal relations hereinafter referred to as "The Lust"), and hereby waives and disclaims any right(s) or entitlement(s) owing in connection with or arising from the Lust, whether such right(s) or entitlement(s) are of a physical, mental, financial, emotional, spiritual, existential, philosophical, subliminal, out-of-body, televised, or other nature.

Signed _____ (The Lover)

(In the Scottish Borders and parts of Cornwall, it is legally sufficient to place the Lover's hoof or paw print on the reverse of this form.)

CIVIL PROCEDURE

If you want to be a litigation lawyer, you need to know about 'civil procedure', which means the rules of court you have to follow when bringing or defending an action. The word 'civil' has nothing to do with behaving like gentlemen. It differentiates the rules that apply to a 'civil' action from those that apply to a 'criminal' action. The latter are what you'll come up against if you stab someone or kerb-crawl (unless you're the DPP).

Civil procedure is easy. You just read the rules for whatever court you happen to be in, and follow them like recipes in a cook book: to start an action, you do A; to defend an action, you do B; If the other side lies, you do X; if your side lies, you do Y. In fact, there are only four concepts tricky enough to merit special attention:

Standing

'Standing' denotes a concrete personal interest in a legal action. It's something you've got to have in order to be heard in court.

Such an interest is easy to prove when you've been run over by an articulated lorry. Your broken legs give you standing. But what if you want to sue Parliament for passing a law which restricts fat people from walking on the pavement during lunch hour? If you're a willowy eight stone, you don't have standing because the law in question doesn't affect you personally. Even going out with a fat person isn't enough. This explains why you get six-year old children as plaintiffs in cases about, for instance, the adequacy of education services provided by a local authority. They haven't a clue what the suits are fighting about, but they've got to be a party to the action because they're the ones with standing.

Jurisdiction

The concept of jurisdiction determines which courts hear which cases. To understand this, cast your mind back to how things worked when you were a child: 'cases' about who should weed the garden probably fell within Dad's 'jurisdiction'; those involving whose turn it was to do the washing-up probably fell within Mum's. If it wasn't clear who had jurisdiction, you engaged in 'forum-shopping' – you went to the one most likely to give you the answer you wanted. It's the same in law.

The basic jurisdictional rule is that small matters are heard in the County Court or Crown Court, while cases of a more serious nature are heard in the High Court or Old Bailey, but there is a degree of choice. Lawyers would generally rather have their cases heard in the High Court or Old Bailey, partly because the judges are better, but mainly because of location and prestige. A lawyer who says he's got a two-week trial in the Old Bailey coming up is telling you what a bigshot he is. A lawyer who says he's going to Woking Magistrates Court for the day is telling you where he's going.

Serving a Writ

Long before you can begin to explain to a court how you were sexually harassed by your lecherous boss, you have to give your boss notice of the action. She's entitled to defend herself. You give her notice by delivering to her, or 'serving' on her, a copy of the Writ of Action.

Service of a writ raises many practical questions. If you go to your boss's house and she won't open the door, how do you effect service? By leaving it on her doorstep? Throwing it through the window? Beating her dog with your belt until she can't stand the pitiful howling and opens up?

One option is to hire an independent agent. A private process server, usually a former bouncer or wrestler,

The important thing in litigation is to have your
Court documents prepared well in advance of the hearing.

will lurk in the shadows of her home until he catches her, invariably scaring her into a heart attack (see *Torts*, page 34).

The problem with private process servers is that they are not known for their reliability. The job doesn't pay that well, and not many people enjoy lurking in the shadows of strangers' homes. They are renowned for tossing writs into the nearest skip or over canal bridges. Then they report back for payment. Because they outweigh you by four stones, you pay up.

Class Actions

Contrary to what you might think, a class action isn't a dispute between people who wear Turnbull & Asser shirts, holiday in Mustique, and adorn their living rooms with racing trophies. It is a lawsuit with lots of people on one side or the other.

Class actions haven't taken off in this country the way they have in the US, partly because of the rule aginst contingency fees. This discourages lawyers from pursuing their God-given right to go "plaintiff-hunting".

There is a disagreement over whether this is a good thing or bad thing, and no one knows how far and when the rules will be relaxed. The debate tends to bring out strong, and often misguided, views. As Rodger Pannone said "There is a lot of emotive rubbish spoken about contingency fees, normally by ex-Lord Chancellors who should be stuffed and preserved for posterity."

In the States, lawyers know which side their muffins are buttered on. Huge contingency fees are a fundamental part of being in practice, and the lawyers that specialise in contingency work have it down to an art form. Wealthy corporate defendants,which they have carefully selected after reviewing annual reports, invariably settle before trial because they know that juries will clobber them, given half a chance. And whenever a big class action settles, you can be sure that each side's lawyers go home with an even larger bag of swag than usual.

Until the law catches up in this country, the sure-fire class actions below, will just have to wait.

CLASS ACTIONS WAITING IN THE WINGS

➤ An action against Lloyd Grossman on behalf of viewers of 'Through the Keyhole' who now speak with fake Oxford accents and drawl the phrase "Whort kind of purrson would lurve hyar?" incessantly.

➤ An action against *For Women* on behalf of all men whose wives/ girlfriends/buddies now consider them to be seriously under-equipped in the trouser department.

➤ An action on behalf of all rail commuters who have tried a Casey Jones hamburger and ruined their clothes in a subsequent vomiting fit.

➤ An action against Nabisco on behalf of all Shredded Wheat eaters who couldn't armwrestle their grandmothers.

➤ An action against Vivienne Westwood on behalf of all women who have bought one of her creations and realised that all they need is a squirting flower in their buttonhole to sign on with Chipperfield's Circus.

➤ An action on behalf of all women who have bought *Impulse* and *still* not scored.

TORTS

If you plan to be a litigation lawyer, you need to master torts as well as civil procedure. Civil procedure tells you *how* to sue someone. Torts tell you *what* to sue him *for*.

The first thing you need to understand is what a tort *is*? If someone stabs you, there are three ways he could get into trouble. Firstly, the CPS could go for him. Stabbing someone is a crime. It has been for years.

Secondly, if you and your assailant had previously exchanged promises not to stab each other, you could sue him for breach of contract. He *promised* not to do it.

Thirdly, you could sue him for carving you up. You could demand payment for your medical bills, your pain and suffering, and the cost of your prosthetic nipple. What is the legal theory on which you could sue him? (You always need a theory.) He has committed a *tort* – in this case the tort of redesigning your anatomical landscape without your consent.

A tort is any wrong you can sue someone for. Except breach of contract – that's called breach of contract.

Once you've got a handle on what a tort *is*, all you have to do to start an action is pick a tort – any tort. If you don't like the selection presently available, feel free to make up your own (explaining it to the judge as a logical step in an already apparent trend in the law.)

The 'One-Bite' Rule

To get you going, consider a classic feature of tort law, the 'One-Bite' Rule. Normally a dog owner is allowed to let his dog run freely about the place. This is considered unobjectionable because dogs are common domestic pets and usually don't bite people, unlike, say, hippopotamuses, which must be securely leashed.

What if your adorable Great Dane, Chewy, tears a forty-stitch gash in your neighbour's right arm? Good old playful Chewy – *you* know he was just being affectionate. But your sourpuss neighbour (now called 'Lefty') doesn't see it that way. He's upset. Can Lefty sue you and win?

No. You were not *negligent*. You had no reason to think Chewy would bite anyone. You did not fail to act like that famous figure of tort law, the 'reasonable man'.

Lefty's gash is just his bad luck, like chewing gum on the bottom of your shoe

But what about Pit Bull terriers. They're known nibblers. In fact, they're considered so uncuddly that they come under special statutory rules. And what about that German shepherd that moved into your street at about the same time your cat disappeared? And what about his dog?

More importantly, what about Chewy, now that he has known vicious propensities? For dogs like Chewy, judges apply the 'One-Bite' Rule: after one bite, you are on notice that the dog is dangerous. If he bites again, you as owner can be held liable – and Chewy could be looking at the ultimate discipline.

The lesson for dog owners is clear. Don't squander that first bite on the postman. Make it count.

The One-Bite Rule
Make that first bite count!

False Imprisonment

Another classic tort, a darling of law professors, is 'false imprisonment'. Contrary to what you might think, this doesn't refer to the situation in which four policemen pounce on you, verbally abuse you, and put you in the cells for a night – because you're coloured and happen to drive a BMW. That's something else, including, if it happens in South London, routine.

No, false imprisonment is what you sue young thugs for when they surround your car and won't let you out. False imprisonment could also be what Lefty sues you for when Chewy chases him up a tree and won't let him down until you call him in for a saucer of tea. The key is impairment of someone else's freedom of movement.

Law professors love to pose the following question: What if someone locks your door for several hours while you're asleep, so that you can't get out, but you don't *know* that you can't get out. False imprisonment?

As an academic matter, who knows? Who cares? As a practical matter, if you have a client in this situation, go for it! Judges (famous for cat-napping) will identify with the sleeping party and be incensed at the thought of someone hanging around outside the door. They'll think "What if I woke up and had to go to the lavatory?"

Res Ipsa Loquitur

If you're going to get a court to award your client money because of someone's tort, you have to convince it that the tort actually happened. Usually you do this by eyewitness evidence: you get the old boy who was sleeping off a bottle of Meths in a nearby alley to swear blind that the Double Decker bus went through a red light at 70 m.p.h. when it hit your client's Mini-Moke.

But what if there were no eyewitnesses? What if the Meths drinker is so far gone that he can't get the story straight? All is not lost. You resort to the doctrine of *Res Ipsa Loquitur.* This is Latin for 'The thing *(res)* speaks *(loquitur)* for itself *(ipsa)*'. Note that the words are out of order. No wonder Latin is a dead language.

The case that gave rise to this doctrine involved a man who was walking along one day, minding his own business, when out of the blue he was hit on the head by a barrel of flour. He didn't see it coming. He just woke up in hospital covered in flour.

He sued the owner of the nearby flour warehouse, insisting that even though no one had seen it happen the owner or one of his employees *must* have negligently let the barrel fall out of the window. How else could the accident have happened?

He won his case. The judge said that in some cases the negligence is so clear from the circumstances that proof isn't necessary. He said "The thing speaks for itself."

The only question is, why did he say it in Latin?

Causation

A final subject you need to understand if you're going to specialise in tort is the concept of 'causation'.

Every event has millions of causes. Supposing your son Crispin is injured when he falls off the new bicycle you gave him for Christmas. Who or what *caused* his injury?

Did the bicycle company cause it by making a defective bike? Did the local council cause it by failing to fill in all those potholes you need a ladder to get out of? Did Chewy cause it by leaping at Crispin with that 'dinner time' look in his eyes?

In theory, causation could be traced all the way back to Jesus for 'causing' you to celebrate Christmas.

The law has evolved the concept of 'proximate' causation to solve this difficulty. According to the doctrine, the most *immediate* cause is the one to which liability is assigned. Like most theoretical solutions to practical problems, proximate causation doesn't really help at all. It just gives judges

a convenient label to use to land whoever they want with the cost of the accident. In this case, the judge would assign liability to the bicycle company – it's the one with the money. Who cares that his wisdom will mean that the bike you scheduled for Crispin's brother Percy next Christmas will cost £10 more?

REAL PROPERTY

Every lawyer should get to grips with the law of real property. It's a bind because it's such a jargon-filled area, and requires virtual fluency in Olde English. When other lawyers try to intimidate you with terms like 'easement', 'seisin' and 'fee tail', you need to be able to come right back at them with even more ludicrous ones like 'frankalmoign' 'burgage tenure' and 'ousterlemain'. When you've shown your semantic mettle, you'll have their respect.

Apart from anything else, understanding real property law is the only way to make sure that when you buy that weekend bolt hole in Somerset, you don't have three hundred anoraks trampling through your flower beds every Sunday afternoon.

Real property comprises two things: (1) Land, earth, soil, dirt, and everything else along those lines except what your potted plant is sitting in and what accumulates between your toes when you've been wearing flip-flops all day; and (2) 'Fixtures' i.e. buildings and other items so large, heavy, or immobile as to be virtually part of the land. This latter category includes darts professionals and every female you're ever likely to meet through a dating agency.

You then have to apply the right labels to these two things: for example, if someone sells you a farmhouse with ten acres of land, you don't just say it's your land; you say that you hold a *'fee simple absolute in possession'*.

And if you want to give a plot of that land to your brother's children (your own children bear an unsettling resemblance to the aerobics teacher at your wife's health club) you don't just scribble your instructions on the back of an envelope. You've got to go through the all the right procedures to convey a *'fee tail interest in the land'*.

There are scores of these labels. They don't make sense. They don't sound like anything you've ever heard of. You've just got to memorise them.

Squatter's Rights

A peculiar but important concept of real property is that you can acquire valid legal title to a piece of land simply by taking it and holding on to it for a long time. This method of acquiring title is known as 'adverse possession'.

It isn't quite as easy as it sounds. Firstly you have to *possess* the land and your possession of it must be 'actual'. If you decide you'd like three feet of your neighbour's garden to square off your croquet lawn, it's not enough just to *proclaim* that the three feet are yours. You have to put up your hoops and start playing.

Secondly, your use must be 'open' and 'hostile'. You can't just sneak on to the lawn at night, wearing dark

clothes and a black balaclava, and have a friend snap a flash photo to prove you were there.

And you can't trick your neighbour by telling him you're just borrowing the land for a while, like a cup of sugar. You have to be claiming it's *yours*. Guard dogs and razor wire would help satisfy this requirement.

Thirdly, your use of the land has to be 'exclusive'. If there are other neighbours trying to get in on the act by, say, growing tomatoes on the plot you're trying to claim, you lose. So do they, for the same reason.

Fourthly, you have to use and be in possession of the land 'continuously'. If you want it that badly, and you're too mean to pay for it, cancel your world cruise. Scratch your tour of duty with the Foreign Legion. Forget your hopes of presenting the Holiday Programme. You've got to *be* there.

Finally, you have to hold the land and satisfy all these other requirements for twenty years. This is the hard part.

This is what keeps you from pitching your tent on your neighbour's lawn with the intention of fighting him off until title changes hands – this and the fact that if he calls the police, you'll spend the night in chokey.

If you *could* fulfill all these requirements, your neighbour's lawn could be yours. You could leave him singing the adverse possession blues.

With the right tactics, and a bit of patience, you could take over the whole of South Kensington. How do you think Grosvenor got Mayfair?

The Rule against Perpetuities

The most irritating feature of real property law is the Rule against Perpetuities. Take that fabulous farm in Devon where your father grew up. Or that super piece of undisturbed beachfront on the Isle of Wight where you've holidayed for years and which you want to make sure stays in the family forever? You can't do it. The Rule against Perpetuities won't let you.

Decreed in 1681, the Rule provides that: '*A contingent future interest which, by any possibility, may not vest within twenty-one years after some life in being, is void in its inception.*'

The main point, according to theologians, is that no one should be able to control a piece of land forever. This means that even if you think St. Paul's Cathedral ought to remain a national monument until the end of time, people in the year 2500 should be able to convert it into a raw sewage plant if they want to.

The Rule against Perpetuities has inspired endless pages of discussion, pages which would have been more usefully employed on perforated rolls in motorway service stations.

If you were studying the Rule in your degree course, this is the sort of situation you would have to apply it to:

'*A makes a gift to B for the life of C, remainder to D's heirs, so long as D has heirs, but if C's first born should be of another species, then to E's heirs, so long as B's grandchildren may reside in Lancashire, then to such heirs of B as may survive the then living residents of Broadmoor.*'

You would have two minutes to answer this question.

CHAPTER FOUR

SUMMER PLACEMENTS

'Flattery and Deception'

Lots of law students spend their summer holidays on a placement with a law firm. Summer placements are not unlike teenage black-tie balls, where you dress like an adult, drink like an adult, and try to get your end away like an adult – only to realise later that it is about as close to real life as Tony Blair is to working class idealism. Oh yes, summer placements resemble private practice, but there are significant differences of which you should be aware.

Socially, they can be pleasant indeed. Most firms, particularly the large ones, wine and dine summer clerks like visiting dignitaries. In the good times these extravagancies were on a par with anything Caligula's party-planners served up, but even in the frugal Nineties you'll be treated to some excellent food – all on Mr. Freeman, of course.

The ulterior purpose of this largesse is to stimulate a serious lust for lucre in the corruptible heart of the law student, and to blind him to the rather grimmer reality of private practice.

As a PR routine, it contains elements of the comical and the fraudulent. *Comical* because of the disparity between the actual contribution of the clerks to the work of the firm and the attention accorded them: few summer clerks do enough useful work to really pay their way, and none of them actually commands the respect of the partners.

Fraudulent simply because it is unrealistic. The conviviality and the largesse is a seasonal phenomenon, lasting for a few short weeks in the Summer, but conspicuously absent the rest of the year. Ask yourself why that partner who strolls through the library says a cheerful hello to you but completely ignores the full-time assistant on the next desk. Does the partner not remember the assistant's name? Did he know his name when he was a summer clerk? Did something change when he signed on permanently?

Most law students save a few

weeks at the end of the summer to travel or work on their tans. This is understandable but unfortunate, because that is when you could get your most realistic look at a firm. By then, the regulars are sick of playing host to presumptious undergraduates, and the facade of rah-rah enthusiasm collapses. The result is normalcy, grim, ugly normalcy. If possible, stick around a while longer – it'll be an eye-opener.

Professionally, as well as socially, summer placements depart from reality. Most firms engage in 'cream-skimming' i.e. reserving for summer clerks all the interesting projects around the office (a big firm may have two or three in a summer). This is why so many summer clerks are later surprised to find that being a trainee offers about as much dignity and satisfaction as sweeping Earls Court after the Horse of The Year Show.

Firms compound the fraud by overlooking mistakes by summer clerks that, if committed by a full-time assistant, would mean the loss of her job or even her dictaphone. This may sound like good news as far as the clerk is concerned, but in reality it's a mixed blessing.

Unless you make a serious hash of things, like misspelling a partner's name in a memo, all you'll be told is that your work was excellent and that everyone liked you. Whichever firm you end up with, you are bound to return to the patterns and practices that served you so well in those few short weeks, only to discover that those patterns and practices are about as acceptable as white socks. By then , you'll be in such a rut that you won't be able to resurrect your career even if you're lead player in the New Testament.

Essential Tools for a Summer Placement

CHAPTER FIVE

THE LEGAL PRACTICE COURSE

'Thousands of Morons have passed. So can you!'

The first decision you confront after graduating with a law degree is whether or not to take up that place at law school you reserved eons ago.

In the past there was a powerful reason for taking the Law Society's Finals course: a pass virtually guaranteed a job with a firm which would train you, pay you, and maybe like you enough to keep you on after qualification. Never mind that you had to sell your soul to the Great God Mogadon for two years. It was worth something in the end, it *led* somewhere.

It's difficult to say that now. The Law Society's grim prediction for 1995-1996 is that one in every three students who pass the LPC will not find a training position with a firm.

To understand how this gross mismatch between supply and demand came about you have to go back to the mid to late 1980s, the years of Big Bang and big billing.

Picture it. 1985. City firms are creaming off vast fees from M&A work and sucking in lawyers from provincial firms to cope with the workload. As that wellspring dries up, the City Fathers realise that they have to home-grow some talent. The cry goes up that not enough quality trainees are being produced by the system and will someone please increase the body count. The polytechnics think (wrongly) that this clarion call is aimed at them and hurriedly set up law courses. Those universities already running courses double capacity. The College of Law establishes a major new facility in York. It's boom time.

And then, almost as suddenly as it arrived, the boom is over. The sky turns dark with chickens coming home to roost. The 1987 Crash has ripped the guts out of City document-factories, and with it the armies of new recruits whose job had been to proofread them. The City Fathers cry Recession! and say that far too many recruits are being produced for their needs. Meantime, High Street firms, reliant on conveyancing work, are floored by the property crash and can barely afford to pay their own partners, let alone low-billing trainees.

It's depression, recession, cyclical downturn, whatever you like to call it, and the last thing anybody wants are moon-faced legal trainees clogging up the corridors.

Unfortunately, no one tells the legal education machine of the changed circumstances. Colleges up and down the country continue to cookie-cut thousands of greenhorn lawyers a year, fed by an apparently limitless supply of students who little realise that they are heading into a profession with no vacancies.

And that's pretty much how it is today. Law remains one of the most popular higher education degrees, and parents still fondly imagine that it is the ultimate safe profession, a "passport to anything". The irony is that for many, it is about as safe and full of promise as being Richard Gere's favourite gerbil.

There are a few points of light amid this picture of gloom. Dame Nature has a way of reducing the procreative excesses of any species, and in this case, local authorities are happy to do the culling for her. Very few of them provide grants for the £5,000 LPC course and, with little prospect of a job to pay off accumulated debts at the end of the course, students without private means are being forcibly excluded from the running. To the extent that that improves the odds for those still in the race, and regardless of meritocratic principle, that's a good thing.

The other encouraging news is the evolution (not before time) of the LPC curriculum itself. Until not so long ago, it was a pure memory test. You could be brain-dead but provided you could learn the order of distribution of a limited partnership's assets and a thousand other heart-breaking rules, you would get through. An ability to think was irrelevant since so many of the rules were completely arbitrary. Either you knew the distribution of a partnership's assets, or you didn't. Not even Edward de Bono could work it out. You just had to sit down and learn them.

Someone twigged that perhaps this wasn't the best way to prepare lawyers for real life. The LPC was changed radically to emphasise practical skills like legal research, client interviewing, and document drafting. There are role-playing sessions in which students learn how to deal face-to-face with the enemy. Between 30% and 50% of the course is subject to continuous assessment. Even the exams are conducted within Amnesty guidelines: students can now take their textbooks in with them and don't have to learn great chunks of statute by heart.

Minimum Critical Effort

The curriculum may have become more candidate-friendly, but some things never change. Finals are still a test, there are still papers to be taken, and it is still possible to fail them. Just because you no longer have to memorise thousand-page casebooks (some come with wheels on) doesn't mean you should lighten up on exam-taking strategy or get complacent. For the exam-sitting part of the course, heed the following:

➤ Your goal is to pass, not to get the highest grade in the year. 'MCE.' should be your guide: Minimal Critical Effort. The ideal grade is the lowest pass of your year.

➤ You will hear stories of people who spent all summer windsurfing in Cannes, glanced at the textbooks on the flight home, and then breezed through the exam. Such stories are like the Monster Raving Loony Party manifesto: appealing but ultimately unrealistic. You have to give Finals *something*.

➤ What if you fail? Failing Finals is not the end of the world, but it *is* undeniably a drag. For one thing, you have to shell out good money to undergo Round 2 retakes. And you'll be doing them in mid-Winter when your co-sufferers won't be wearing skimpy summer clothes and nice tans to keep your morale up.

Also, the whole world will know. In the first place national newspapers publish the names of everybody who has passed, and people (especially relations) pore over the list the same way they pore over the fatalities from a major train crash, as interested in the names that *aren't* on it as those that are.

And then, when the results come out, some idiot invariably roars down the corridor at your firm (you should have started as a trainee by then) shouting "I did it! I passed! Thank God! Oh Thank God!" And then everybody turns to you to see why you're not similarly jubilant.

➤ So how can you avoid failing? There is one golden rule: Don't Panic! People get nervous about Finals, for understandable reasons: the physical environment is unfamiliar; the people around you are strangers; the exam invigilator can't find your name on his list. But don't let butterflies turn into full-blown panic. There's no reason why you should: you've taken hundreds of exams before, and these ones are different only in length. Remind yourself that you have never failed an exam in your life. If you *have* failed an exam in your life, remind yourself that no one has ever been jailed for failing Law Finals. (First offenders usually get a suspended sentence.)

Qualifications aren't *everything* but the profession retains a quaint respect for their significance. If only someone had told John Darlow. Darlow, a man with no legal qualifications, masqueraded as a solicitor for 17 months, on one occasion representing a client in court, before being found out. He even allowed his law firm to throw a champagne reception to celebrate his 'admission' to the roll. He now drives taxis for a living. The charging system, at least, is familiar.

At the end of the seventh day, when the final "Put down your pens" has been called, you will feel giddy, like a marathon runner crossing the finishing line*. This is partly because of all the nervous energy you will have expended. You may also have forgotten to eat for several days. At this point you should do three things:

Firstly, go home and get some sleep. Fatigue contributes to depression. When you wake up, you will have only the vaguest memories of the agony you have been through.

Secondly, resist talking about the exam. (If you still need to be told this after all these years, you are an incorrigible jerk. View this as one last chance to redeem yourself.)

Thirdly, take as long a holiday as you can possibly afford. Once you start work, you may not have a similar opportunity for decades.

You will not get your Finals results for three or four months. The inherent horribleness of this delay will be exacerbated by rumours about lost exam papers, unprecedented failure rates, and cheating scandals that require everyone to take the exams again. Ignore them. The same ones surface year after year – apparently by spontaneous generation – although Creationists decry this secular view.

The important thing to remember is that you will eventually pass. If not the first time, the second, If not the second, the third. What you really need to worry about is what comes after that.

---

*You may also smell a bit funky – the analogy with the marathon runner is again apt.

COPING WITH FEAR: CONTINUE TO WRITE

You don't have to be a naturally timid person to experience fear during Law Finals. You can easily pick it up from someone else.

Fear is contagious. When the person next to you starts emiting regular and powerful rectal sobs, you may find your own stomach begins to churn. This is understandable, like the feeling you get when the pilot of your aeroplane emerges from the cockpit strapping on his parachute.

Suppress your feeling of panic. Continue to write. *Whatever happens*, continue to write. If your neighbour has a heart attack, continue to write. If *you* have a heart attack, try to guts it out until the invigilator calls an end to the exam. If you can't last that long, be sure to gasp loudly or wave your arms to catch the invigilator's attention because those around you with any sense will carry on writing.

PRACTICAL SKILLS THEY OUGHT TO TEACH
YOU IN LAW SCHOOL – *BUT DON'T*

➢ Faking interest during interviews.

➢ Not believing ninety per cent of what they tell you when you do a summer placement at a firm.

➢ Masking your delight at the size of your first pay slip.

➢ Masking your disappointment at the size of your twenty-fifth pay slip.

➢ Dealing with sexual advances by senior lawyers.

➢ Dealing with sexual advances by senior lawyers' wives.

➢ Sucking up to secretaries and other support staff.

➢ Pretending you don't think your clients are stupid.

➢ Sleeping with your eyes open. (Hey, fish do it.)

➢ Not worrying about the cost to your client.

➢ Generating excuses for monumental errors.

➢ Mediating between your brain's craving for coffee and your bowels' craving for peace.

➢ Pretending you don't hate everyone at your firm.

➢ Pretending you don't regret going into law.

If all else fails, what's a little begging
when your career's at stake?

CHAPTER SIX

RECRUITING

"I spent £250 on a new suit just to meet this dwork?"

Time was when a law student could stroll into Slaughter & May on a Friday afternoon, say "So what can you lot do for me?" and, provided the stud in her nose wasn't too obvious, she'd be behind her desk on Monday morning.

Those days are but a distant memory. Articles, or 'training contracts' as they're now called, are rarer than rocking-horse shit, with dozens of qualifiers chasing every one vacancy this year. And it's going to get worse before it gets better.

In such a competitive climate, success and failure depends as much on inter-personal skills as academic ability. And the crunch comes at interview time. You can't afford to breeze in and out of them any more, treating the first two or three tiddlers as warm-ups for the biggies at the end. You can't rely on your natural charm, wit and evident intelligence to pull you through when the questioning gets tough. You've got to treat interviews

as the sternest most intensive test of all, and do your homework accordingly.

Because let's face it, getting a job is what it's all about. Not many people go to law school because they can't think of anything else to do with their money.

Interviews have a lot in common with family weddings. Both involve forced smiles, frequent handshakes, questions that no one cares about the answers to, and a radical departure from normal behaviour. As with weddings, you need to tailor your performance to the occasion.

The way you present yourself to a City firm which advises financial institutions and mega-rich private clients is going to be very different from the way you present yourself to a small High Street firm which does criminal and personal injury work for legally-aided clients. Lawyers in these firms are in the profession for entirely different reasons and, given that everybody recruits in their own

"Nice guys but an odd firm. They practise the law of the jungle."

image, your strategy should be to mirror the attitudes and appetites which the partners display.

If you don't know what kind of firm you're interviewing at check the directories like Chambers and The Legal 500. Failing that, its location can be a good indication, because firms tend to hang around their client bases. Entertainment law firms are usually in the West End, computer law firms in the M4 corridor, and white collar crime firms as close as they can get to stockbrokers.

It used to be that the only place for ambitious commercial lawyers was the City of London. London is still dominant but not overwhelmingly so. Read on.

Over the last five years London has been under sustained attack from a determined phalanx of regional firms from Leeds, Manchester and Brum. These firms are posing a serious threat to the second tier of medium-sized City firms and arguably to the first tier too. The reason is simple. They charge less than City firms. They can afford to do this because their office and staff overheads are much lower.

The quality of their work is, they claim, just as good. With stunning countryside on their doorsteps, and house prices thirty per cent lower than London, they have no trouble at all pinching highly-skilled assistants from City firms.

Leading the regional challenge is the Yorkshire firm, Dibb Lupton, which has increased its fee income fivefold since 1989 and which revels in its image as rottweiler of the profession. In 1990 it opened an office near Moorgate. "It was a statement about the firm in London," says their managing partner, Paul Rhodes. "We are here, we are serious, and we mean business."

Publicly, the City firms shrug off the challenge. Privately, they fear and resent it. "People make the sign of the cross to you at cocktail parties. The mark of the beast" says Stuart Denson, Dibb Lupton's Head of Business Development. He should know how they feel. Before joining Dibb Lupton he was top fee earner at Turner Kenneth Brown.

Whichever kind of firm you want to work for, there are common ground rules to observe if you want to get the job.

The main rule to bear in mind is that law firms, like lemmings, have no independent sense of judgement. They want you if they think their competitors want you. They are less interested in your credentials than in how their competitors view your credentials. *Ergo* – your goal is to make them think that other leading firms have already made you an offer or are on the verge of doing so.

This doesn't mean you actually have to lie. You can achieve the desired effect simply by dropping the names of other big firms into the conversation – what you think of Clifford Chance's training programme, how Herbert Smith's fancy offices struck you, why you're not sure whether Linklaters is for you. If anyone asks if these firms have actually made you an offer, you can say that you haven't heard from them yet – which is particularly true if you've never even had an interview with them.

In order to land the job , you will probably have to survive two types of contact: the on-campus screening and the full-scale assault at the firm's offices. Each of these calls for different strategies and techniques.

The On-Campus Screening

Most of the big firms give presentations at what they regard as the acceptable universities. Oxford and Cambridge. Some of them make a self-conscious effort to broaden the intake by visiting Bristol too. If you're at some third-rate university, forget it. They won't even have heard of you.

Assuming you attend one of these presentations, what should your tactics be, bearing in mind that the room is likely to be full to the brim with other finalists equally desperate to make an impression, first-year students hoping for some free booze, and a student band rehearsing speed riffs?

The conventional approach will not work. Thrusting your CV into a visiting partner's hand, when he's already trying to balance a paper plate of cocktail sausages and vol-au-vents will only serve to irritate.

Neither is this the occasion to dazzle him with stories of past academic triumphs.

At the on-campus presentation, you have to score your points on *personal style*, rather than substantive qualities. This means more than wearing matching shoes, doing your flies up, and remembering the name of the firm in which you're supposedly eager to spend the rest of your professional career, important as those things are. (If you show up in an Umbro shell suit you might as well make the most of the free grub, because that's all you'll get out of the evening.) It means being distinctive, memorable. It means not boring the hell out of the visiting partner with weak questions that you should already know the answers to ("How big is your firm?") or that the partner couldn't care less about ("Does the luncheon voucher entitlement increase with inflation?") or which show you're labouring under some terrible misapprehension ("Me and my girlfriend want to go to the same firm, and work in adjacent offices. Will that be possible at your firm?")

It means asking questions not about the firm, but about the visiting partner personally ("Did you have any expectations when starting at the firm that weren't met?"), so he'll have an opening to talk about the subject that interests him most, namely, himself. The applicant who does this is invariably remembered as 'a stimulating, thoughtful, conversationalist'.

Do some homework on the firm in advance so that you can impress the partner with the incisiveness of your questions. Crawfords Directory of City Connections lists the quoted clients of all the major law firms.

If you know which partner is going to be visiting, try to find out a bit about him, and drop complimentary references to his university, his place of birth and the year he was born. Legalese, publishers of The 'Legal 500', put out an occasional supplement on individuals which includes mug shots and brief biographical details of the bigger swinging dicks.

But be tactful with this 'informed' approach. The partner won't enjoy talking about the recent SFO raid on his firm's offices, not will he care to speculate on his son's chances of parole.

Finally, if you have any choice in the matter, try to attend a presentation early on in the milk round, when the visiting partners are still feeling fresh and don't feel like they're going to throw up if they see one more eager beaver in a new suit who really has no idea what he's getting into.

The Formal Interview

The vital thing to remember about the formal interview is to go easy on the coffee. Quite apart from the fact that you may be too nervous to hold the cup steadily, every firm will offer you some, and you simply cannot win the battle of the bladder.

Otherwise your strategy should be straight out of *"How to Win Friends and Influence People"*: Talk about whatever your interviewers find most interesting. For lawyers, this means talking about themselves. It isn't hard to get them going. Ask what kind of law they practise, how long they've been at it, what got them into it.

GROOMING YOURSELF FOR INTERVIEW

One of the trickier areas on which to make recommendations, because there's a limit to what you can do if your face doesn't fit. You may be the best legal brain of your year, but if you look like you're about to offer your interviewer £2,000 worth of the leading export commodity of Bogota, he'll get nervous. Neverthless, there are various elements of appearance that you should be aiming for. With work and a bit of practice, you can get surprisingly good results from even unpromising physical material.

Eyes

Must be purposeful and thoughtful, with just the right number of blinks per minute. Eye colour is less important as most people don't notice anyway; blue-grey is probably the ideal, but anything other than cockerel-orange will do.

Mouth

Short of dribbling onto your tie or leering like Rik Mayall, you should be alright with whatever kisser God gave you. If you plan to be a litigator, however, add a hint of ruthlessness to your appearance by pursing your lips occasionally in a thin smile.

Complexion

If you've picked up a tan in the course of your summer revision,white it out before you go for interview. Law firms have a strong aversion to tans, which they've heard are acquired doing unnatural things like swimming, windsurfing, and playing golf – anywhere, in fact, but in library basements.

If on the morning of your interview you're looking just too damn drop-dead hunky, take immediate action. Shaving with a bread knife, or chew some cordite in the train like Edward Fox did in The Day of the Jackal. It will render your skin an instant lawyerly grey.

Expression

Decisive, authoritative, cynical, manipulative, calculating, are some of the descriptions to go for. A tall order for one face, granted, especially while tackling Eyes and Mouth at the same time, so take it slowly. Start with a couple at a time, and work your way up.

Interviews are no time to be shy. Law firms like assertiveness in their trainees.

Lawyers love contemplating their origins and destinies.

Towards the end of the interview, throw in a question or two about the firm and its excellent reputation, just to show you're a serious player. You'll strike a particularly responsive chord if you inject references to 'billings' or 'profits' – anything related to money.

If you fall short of conversation, personalise the discussion. He may have a framed picture of himself and some celebrity client on the wall. Ask him how he got to know Tarby or Placido. He won't be irritated by your impudence. Why do you think the pictures are on the wall in the first place?

On the other hand, you're probably better off *not* complementing the old geezer on the lovely picture of his grandaughter sitting on his desk – it'll only turn out to be his fourth wife.

If you're being interviewed by an assistant rather than a partner (it's amazing how often partners fail to turn up) the rules are rather different. Don't bother asking about the firm at all. He's probably just put down an armful of legal documents with page numbering in three figures. The last thing he wants to talk about is more law.

Take note of the trappings of his office. The things he has on display are things he likes to talk about, things he's proud of. If he has an oar hanging on the wall, ask him if by chance he ever crewed an eight at University. (Be sure to say 'crewed an eight' rather than 'rowed a boat'. Rowers are a quaint breed and even fussier about terminology than lawyers.)

If on the other hand he's Mr Puniverse's weedy cousin, steer the conversation towards 'safe' subjects like bidding conventions in contract bridge, or your long-held ambition to holiday with the Navajo Indians. He's bound to have similar interests.

At some point in the interview, express curiosity as to whether the partnership recognises the talents of its star assistants (including, by clear implication, the one you're talking to). Every assistant feels under-valued, and this comment will render you instantly likeable in his eyes.

The Recruiting Lunch

Sometimes, the recruiting ritual includes an expensive lunch. When you're an indigent student, this can be a major occasion, both as your first square meal in weeks, and as your first taste of legal largesse.

In the right frame of mind, a recruiting lunch can be fun. Your hosts will usually be assistants rather than partners, and if they've got any sense they will take full advantage of the outing to enjoy themselves and run up a hefty bill at the partners' expense.

A recruiting lunch can also be an opportunity to get the truth about a firm, depending on how many drinks the assistants have had and whether they're the sort who feed on another's gripes. "You think *you* got shafted by Emslie? Listen to what the bastard did to *me* last week . ." Encourage them to continue in this vein.

If they offer you a drink, do you accept? Of course you do – *you* don't have to go back to work. This is especially true if your hosts are already three sheets to the wind. You don't want to be a stuck-in-the-mud.

What should you order? This is not the time to play 'Stump the Barman'. Order wine – it's classier than Special Brew. And don't look surprised when the waiter asks if you want red or white. Wine always comes in colours.

Above all don't feel guilty about the cost of the meal, or try to minimise the bill by underordering. It's not *your* fault they're trying to impress you and they won't thank you for ordering the cheapest pasta dish on the menu. Just view it as part of your reward for accumulating a good record. Besides, whatever firm you end up with will extract recompense soon enough.

Your Curriculum Vitae

Don't waste your time producing a flashy CV. Lawyers are not aesthetic enough to appreciate good packaging, and view a really slick-looking CV with scepticism, even scorn. They just aren't into glitz; they're into drab, which they think shows them to be people of substance rather than mere form.

What they are really interested in are your exam results. Occasionally they might consider other achievements which show an unusual ability to stomach huge piles of grunt work – if, for instance, you have worked as a proofreader with a Sanskrit publisher, or spent summer holidays shoveling stable strudel at your local riding school. These kinds of activities say something about your suitability for legal practice.

If your exam results are good, put them front and centre. That's obvious. The problem is what to do

RECRUITING LUNCH DISASTERS

No matter how relaxed a recruiting lunch may seem, remember that you are on trial. Don't try to be funny, by for example unscrewing the top of the salt cellar and offering it to your host, no matter how many rounds of applause that particular stunt won you in your campus refectory. And beware of these common mistakes:

➢ At a Chinese restaurant, don't blow your nose on the pancakes that come with the Peking Duck.

➢ At an Italian restaurant, don't order spaghetti bolognese or any other dish likely to get friendly with the front of your shirt.

➢ At *any* restaurant, avoid exotic dishes like cat or raw boa-constrictor. Only seriously deranged litigators at Herbert Smith are expected to enjoy these, and then only on the eve of a major court case.

➢ Resist the temptation to pop one of those round yellow tasty-looking things into your mouth. It is probably a butterball. And if you do make this mistake, don't try to rescue the situation by declaring "Now *that's* what I call a good butterball."

➢ If the bill passes within your visual range, do not let out a long low whistle and exclaim "Hey, I didn't know we broke a window!"

with them if they're execrable? What if the only A-grade you got was in one of those touchy-feely social science subjects where *everybody* got an A, because the bearded tree-hugger who taught it didn't like passing negative value judgements?

It's a tricky one. Your interviewer isn't just passing the time when he asks about your exam results. If yours are dreadful you have two options: the first is to look him in the eye and assert with cool confidence "These marks don't reflect what I can do"

and hope they fall for it. (Be sure to say "*these* marks"rather than "*my* marks". The goal is to disassociate yourself from them, as if they were somebody else's.)

The other option is to look him in the eye and assert with cool confidence "My father is a rich and powerful man. He'd be very pleased indeed if you took me on".

History suggests the second is the more effective ploy.

Two items should not be included in your CV. Firstly, in describing a previous summer placement (if you've done one) don't bother saying 'Researched & drafted memoranda and performed other litigation tasks'. Lawyers know what summer clerks do and it's not impressive enough to warrant elaboration.

Secondly, don't clog up the personal section of your CV with things like 'Health: Excellent'. Law firms don't care about your health. Take a look at the people interviewing you, with their paunches, skinny arms and pasty complexions. Is *their* health excellent?

The Covering Letter

All a covering letter needs to say is "Here's my CV. Can I have a job?" You can dress it up a little with the more formal "Enclosed is my CV" language, but forget the stuff about how you're applying to the firm because it has a varied practice that you believe would offer a stimulating and challenging introduction to a career in the law.

Cut to the chase. You don't have to sell them on their own firm. As a rule, if you have something to say, say it in your CV rather than in the covering letter. There are a few rare exceptions. You might for instance mention in a covering letter that your mother speaks well of the firm – and she should know because she's its biggest client.

Photos

Sometimes firms ask you to attach a photo to your CV. This is so they can identify you at reception, and has nothing to do with wanting to check your race, sex, or class before inviting you in for interview.

Sure.

Do what they say, anyway. Spend an afternoon in a Photo-Me booth trying to get something acceptable. In that first elimination stage, where one hundred CVs make it straight into the 'No' letter tray, and ten go through to the next round, a lot will depend on whether you look the part.

Don't go over the top by, for instance, getting a professional to take a posy shot of you reading Charlesworth in your gazebo, galloping on your pet camel over the South Downs, or staring wistfully at the sunset. Not unless you want to become the office pin-up. Firms aren't looking for 'mood'. They're looking for something forensic, something which will allow them to tell how much alcohol you're likely to have in your bloodstream on a Monday morning, and whether you'll flip when asked to do some Saturday proofreading on a big flotation document *in lieu* of joining your wife on a honeymoon.

Recruiting Letters

Every recruiting letter has one of three basic messages: "Yes", "Maybe", or "When hell freezes over". If you get the last of these, you needn't worry yourself any further. But if the letter says "Yes" or "Maybe" you need to read between the lines to know where you really stand. The examples overleaf show you how.

THE YES LETTER

What the firm *said*:

Waite, Pay, & Pray
1 Midas Avenue
London EC2A 4JD

Mr James Clarke   July 5th 1995
Hodgson Hall,
Exeter University
Devon

Dear Mr Clarke

It was a pleasure to meet you last week. You would clearly fit in well with
this firm and, on behalf of my partners, I would like to offer you a position
as a trainee starting in September 1995.

If you would like to visit our offices and meet some more of our lawyers, do
please call my secretary, Lucy Brader, to arrange a mutually convenient
time.

I look forward to seeing you again.

Yours sincerely,

Hamish Wilson

What the firm *said*:

Waite, Pay, & Pray
1 Midas Avenue
London EC2A 4JD

Mr James Clarke   July 5th 1995
Hodgson Hall,
Exeter University
Devon

Dear Mr Clarke

For someone who started off at an inner-city comprehensive, you've certainly managed to pull yourself up by your bootstraps. Your pale complexion, emaciated physique and overall nerdiness, combined with your consistently brilliant exam results, suggest that you are just the sort of compulsive library-loving swot we're looking for.

No doubt you'll get lots of other offers, because hard-core zealouts like you don't grow on trees. Someone so patently willing to sacrifice his health and social life is a real find.

I wouldn't want to introduce you to a client or have a meal with you, but I bet you could rack up enough billable hours in a year to reduce your salary to the equivalent of £1.95 per hour.

I hope we can sign you up.

Yours sincerely,

Hamish Wilson

THE MAYBE LETTER

What the firm *said:*

Cower Cringe & Tremble
120 Finsbury Avenue
London EC14HB

Ms Georgina Rose   July 5th 1995
Nelson Hall
University of Westhampton
NH1 2GX

Dear Ms Rose

Thank you for coming in to see me last week. I enjoyed our meeting very much. Although I am not able to make you an immediate offer of employment, I know that other partners of the firm would like to meet you for a second interview.

If you are interested in pursuing this invitation, please call our recruitment co-ordinator, Mr Alan O'Flynn, to arrange a mutually convenient time for your visit. You might find it helpful to co-ordinate your visit with interviews at other firms in the City.

Yours sincerely,

Janine Robinson

THE MAYBE LETTER

What the firm *meant:*

Cower Cringe & Tremble
120 Finsbury Avenue
London EC1 4HB

Ms Georgina Rose   July 5th 1995
Nelson Hall
University of Westhampton
NH1 2GX

Dear Ms Rose

I was astonished that someone like you – a mediocre student at a second-rate poly, sorry university – would even bother to apply to Cower Cringe & Tremble. By any standards you're a pitiful specimen.

On the other hand, a bald willingness to ask for something you have no right to is worth a lot in this profession. You couldn't possibly have a real future with us, but we always need more bodies, and we can bill your time at the same rates as our decent trainees. Clients can't tell the difference.

I'm not willing to take sole responsibility for hiring you, so you'd better come in and see a few more of our people. Unless you can persuade some other firm to pick up the tab, you're going to have to thumb your way down.

Yours sincerely,

Janine Robinson

Recruiting Misrepresentations

Law firms, like secondhand car dealers, are known for their willingness to misrepresent reality. Their recruitment brochures often deviate so far from the truth as to constitute what most people would call 'lies'.

Lies told by law firms and car dealers are not punishable under the law. They're known as 'mere puffs'. Examples of puffing by car salesmen would be "There will always be a strong resale market for the Allegro" and "the Robin is well-known for its road-holding". Below are some of the most common recruiting lies, each translated into what recruiters *would* say if they were burdened by a proclivity for the truth.

What Recruiters *Say*	What Recruiters *Mean*
Our assistants work hard, but like it.	Our assistants work hard.
You'll get an excellent training at this firm.	At the end of your training, you'll have the skills of a legal secretary.
We have one of the more diversified practices in the City.	We take any work that comes in the door.
We believe in lean staffing of cases.	We make each assistant do the work of three.
We don't spend the entire day in the office.	We take a lot of work home.
Our lawyers maintain a variety of outside interests.	Three years ago we had an assistant whose wife played the piano.
This firm likes to keep a low profile.	Nobody has ever heard of us.
We encourage pro bono work.	We tolerate pro bono work on weekends.
We believe in bringing trainees along one step at a time.	You'll be indexing court documents for months on end.
We have a policy of carefully controlled growth.	We're losing clients.

HARD QUESTIONS

One of the mistakes law students make is that they try to be *nice*. This is a misconceived strategy in any interview, but particularly so in the law, where deference is seen as a weakness and an ability to stand up for yourself an absolute must.

Instead of rolling over and having your tummy tickled, you should show them what you are made of by tossing in a few 'hard' questions of your own. You need to know the answers anyway, and the interviewers will respect you for asking them.

• How does the firm decide on assistants' salaries? Are they pegged to 'productivity' (ie billed hours)? If so, does the calculation include all the hours spent doing things that assistants are frequently asked to do but get no credit for?

• How many assistants have left the firm in the past year?

• What kind of training does the firm give trainees? Is it all 'on the job'? i.e. zilch.

• Are any assistants presently working on a single big case, and if so how long have they been on it? Will *you* be assigned to it?

• Did most (all) of the partners go to public school? How many of them talk with anything other than an Oxford English accent?

• How many hours does the average assistant bill each year? (This figure should be lower than the total number of hours in a year.)

• Are all trainees automatically offered jobs when they qualify, and do they have a choice as to which department they join? (Many firms are retaining only 70% of this year's qualifiers.)

• Does the firm have non-equity partners? ie 'partners' who are paid a fixed salary rather than a share of the profits (Non-equity partnership is a sham device for postponing the day of real partnership, in many cases indefinitely.)

• Ask your interviewers – especially the ones you like – if they will still be at the firm one year from now. You don't want to arrive to find that all the good guys have left town.

• If you fail one of more of your Finals papers, will your firm give you:

(a) Time off for retakes on full pay?

(b) Time off for retakes without pay?

(c) All the time you want for retakes and your P45?

CHAPTER SEVEN

HOW TO SURVIVE
(AND MAKE PARTNER)
IN YOUR LAW FIRM

*'You can make it if you know
what to kiss and whose'*

Every day being an assistant solicitor in a large law firm is like walking a tightrope over shark-infested waters: one wrong step could mean the end. Most assistants walk this tightrope with their eyes wide shut.

Survival is the name of the game, and in order to survive in a law firm, it is critical to keep in mind one simple truth: the partners run the show.

Admittedly, some of them run more of it than others, and the idea, which they hold out to the public, that all partners regard each other as equals is as accurate as saying that the Gabon is the equal of the USA because they're both sovereign states, or that a 1964 E-Type is the same as a Chieftain Tank because they both have the same m.p.g.

The main point as far as you are concerned is that partners are tenured and you're not. It is hard to get rid of them – and easy to get rid of you. Therefore your goal must be to cultivate their approval.

Over time this cultivation may become odious to you. As one assistant commented: "They should make my senior partner Pope. That way all I'd have to kiss is his ring."

Assuming you can stomach the thought of prolonged obsequiousness, how can you ensure that the partners will vote thumbs-up when your name comes up for partnership eight or nine years down the road?

There are two reasons why a partner would vote to bring you into the club: (1) he likes you, and (2) he thinks you'll make him rich.

Practically speaking, he may like

you *because* he thinks you'll make him rich – a not uncommon confluence of motivations. Just remember that great warm-nosed dog you had as a child, which nuzzled up to you and wagged its tail when it saw you coming – as long as you continued to feed it.

Try to think of the partners as large furry Labradors with unusually strong appetites.

In order to make the partners like you, you need to make them think you're *like* them, that you're one of them. You even want them to think of you as a surrogate son or daughter (unlike their actual sons and daughters who live in squats, and play the social security system for a living). Also, in order to make the partners think you'll make them rich, you need to cast yourself in their own preferred self-image: ultra professional and workaholic.

To succeed in this dual quest, there are a number of very specific rules that you must follow. These are key maxims that you should tape to your bathroom mirror for review each morning as you tie your tie or trim your nose hairs.

Strict adherence to these rules could, in time, get you a window office with a secretary who will type one-page letters and pass on phone messages within several days of a call being made. Deviation from them could land you in a basement office across from the postroom, sharing a surly secretary whose idea of good service is not chewing her Orbit Sugar-free too loudly when she listens in on your private telephone calls.

Rule 1: *Cover Your Arse*

This rule is the most important of all the rules, as well as the most difficult to observe. The reason it is difficult to observe is that its command embraces everything you do, no matter how trivial. A discussion of all the applications of this rule could fill several volumes, but some examples will suffice:

Supervise everything that your secretary sends out in the post

The stories of letters going out in the wrong envelopes are legion. If your secretary mixes up the memo you intended for your client, in which you point out that his gold bullion sales in Switzerland "might have consequences for his capital gains liability", with a letter to the Inland Revenue, saying your client has nothing to report, you might as well start clearing your desk.

Proofread everything – carefully

This is particularly important when a partner hands you a document and says "Take a quick look at this and then put it in the post." He might very well think it's okay when he gives it to you, but . . . in that case why is he giving it to you? What you're seeing is an instinctive effort to cover *his* arse. If a legal argument proves to have been stated inaccurately, or the numbers just don't add up, you can be certain that the next document you proofread will be your CV.

THE OPEN-DOOR POLICY

"We welcome constructive criticism from articled clerks and assistants"

Law firms love to boast of their openness to criticism and reform. They claim to observe an open-door policy with respect to grievances from articled clerks and assistants, and express an eagerness to hear suggestions from below.

Such claims should be taken with more salt than you'll find in a Cerebos warehouse. Once you get to your firm, try them out. Suggest keeping the heating on during Winter weekends, because it's difficult to write wearing skiing gloves. Ask for soft loo paper i.e. something less corrosive than computer paper, in the lavatories.

The response from any partner you approach will be "I'm glad you brought that one up, Sandra. You know, it was a problem when I was an assistant. Yes, it's certainly a problem." This is intended to convey the message "I know how you feel. I'm a regular guy." It also conveys the message "I'm not going to do anything about it. No one is. Take it like a man."

So much for the open-door policy. But why don't assistants band together in committees to represent their views on a formal basis to partners. In other words, unionise? Well, they do ... and they don't.

The basic problem is *ambition*. Assistants see no long-term benefit in improving their lot, because they don't intend to *be* assistants five years down the road. They plan to become part of the management.

The pragmatic way is to take it on the chin, and wait for the day when you're the one dispensing the favours. Until then, hang on to your skiing gloves and your personal roll of Andrex.

Before sending out a document, clear it with someone senior to yourself

The point is to place responsibility for a mistake anywhere but on your shoulders. Not only should you run a document past a senior person, but you should also dictate a file memo saying that you have done so, and somehow let an *even more senior* person know you've cleared the document with the person in between.

Notify and consult the client about everything you do on his case

Clients don't affect you directly, but they are more than capable of moaning about your performance to partners, and in rare instances they will even get upset enough to sue the firm.

Your aim should be to build a record – consisting of letters to the client covering *everything* – to make it look as if it is he who is responsible for any disasters that occur.

Partners, you will find, are the ultimate arse-coverers in this way, spending hours of billable time drafting letters explaining to the client why the firm is doing what it is doing. This could all be done by telephone for one-tenth of the expense, but such an approach would reduce billings and – even worse – leave the firm's collective arse uncovered.

In reporting meetings on your time sheets, factor in an unknown

Never just write "Attended meeting with Counsel: 1 hour". Far too precise. If a partner was there, she might have recorded the meeting on her time sheet as lasting only forty minutes. Even if you were the only lawyer present, the client might complain to a partner that he thought the meeting only lasted forty minutes. In either case, the discrepancy could be very damaging to your reputation. You'll never be given the opportunity to prove that you were the only sober, non-hallucinating, non-schizophrenic person present.

Always write: *"Prepared for and attended meeting with Counsel: 1 hour"*. Those three extra words, which cost you nothing, could make all the difference.

The same principle applies when you've spent all day proofreading hundreds of pages of Swap Agreements. It's not as if you did anything wrong. You were *supposed* to spend all day proofreading those things. But dress it up a little. Instead of saying "Proofreading: 9 hours", say, *"Reviewing, editing and* proofreading: 9 hours". Again, three little words that make all the difference.

Before starting work on a file make sure you understand what the partner wants

This is not as easy as it sounds. The partner might want an assertive piece that contains no reference to any authority running against the client's position. He might want a general survey of the law, including all authorities whether favourable or unfavourable. He might initially want the latter, but having read your analysis, decide he wants the former, and wonder why you didn't give it to him in the first place. Rarely will he *tell* you what he wants. You've got to guess.

This raises the question of what your immediate response should be

PUT THE BURDEN ON THE CLIENT

When writing to a client to request that he "verify" and sign an affidavit that you have drafted, don't be too proud to include some weasly (yet lawyerly) words like the following:

'Please read, review, examine, and consider all aspects of this document thoroughly and thoughtfully. Needless to say, you are perfectly, totally, and absolutely free to make any additions, alterations, corrections, amendments, clarifications, enhancements, breast augmentations, or even changes that you feel are appropriate, necessary, desirable, worthwhile, or good. Thereafter, and only thereafter, if it meets with your full and complete satisfaction, agreement, approval and liking, sign it and . . .'

When you include this sort of material, the *client* is responsible for whatever you've produced, and your arse is covered. (For God's sake, keep a copy of your correspondence.)

when a partner presents you with instructions so garbled that you suspect his sobriety. As a rational person, you will be tempted to ask questions. You will want to clarify the problem and make sure you understand what is required from you.

Resist this impulse. One or two questions are okay, three at most, just to let the partner know you're awake and paying attention as he drones on. (Stifle yawns at all costs)

But no more. Further inquiry, however reasonable, will only make him nervous about your intelligence and legal acumen. If he hasn't made the problem clear the first time round, it's because he doesn't understand it himself.

Your best approach, even in the face of the most wildly confused instructions, is to smile, nod your head, and say "Yes, I see", "I understand". When he has finished (as far as you can tell) leave the office, find a quiet place to vomit, and then track down a senior assistant to tell you what the hell is going on.

Save all your Drafts

It doesn't matter whether you're working on a £100 million oil platform lease, a £2,500 personal injury pleading, or a time-filling memo to put on file. If you show it to a partner (and you should), and he makes you amend it ten or twelve times (and he will), save every version. There's at least a fifty-fifty chance that the partner will call you three days later and say "By the way, Seager, you did save those early drafts, didn't you?"

This makes no sense whatsoever. If you asked the partner why he wanted them, he would say you never know when some of the material in them might prove useful. But the real reason is that he's scared – not of anything in particular; just scared – like a child at night who insists that his father shine a torch under the bed.

Resist pointing out the absurdity of his request. Humour him. Tell him you've saved every scrap, and they're all just waiting for the time when they might be needed. And make sure they are: you never know when he might show up with a torch to check under the bed.

Make five times as many copies of every document as you can possibly use

This is particularly important for litigation documents, for which you will need:

• an original + copies for filing

• another copy that the court will 'file stamp' and return to you so that you can prove that you actually filed it.

• 'service copies' for serving on each of the other parties.

• 'intra-office copies' – send one to every lawyer who has ever had anything to do with the case.

• 'client copies' – send one to everyone at the client's offices who you've talked to, or who you've heard might be interested in the case.

• your own copy.

• fifteen copies for people you have never heard of, but who will materialise out of the woodwork as soon as you have sent the file down to be archived, asking for copies they will never read.

• ten copies to replace the ten that will turn out to have missing pages or that your secretary will have used to clean dog doings off the bottom of her shoe.

• ten copies just to have around, so you can truthfully answer in the affirmative when a partner asks if you made some extra copies in case of an emergency.

This last point is especially important. If you do not make a ridiculous number of extra copies, the partner in charge will find out and be irritated that you did not make a ridiculous number of extra copies.

Also, and most often overlooked, you should get the client to sign *several* copies of everything you may need to file that requires his signature. The reason is that if you don't, and the original is lost, someone will have to crawl to the client for a second signature. It is a weasly precaution, of course, and clued-up clients will be irritated. There is a better than evens chance, however, that some partner will ask if you had the good sense to get extra signed copies, and you will need the tangible proof at hand.

Make extra copies of everything!
It could save your legal career.

Rule 2

Take on as few Files as Possible

This rule may seem inconsistent with what you've heard about the brutal hours assistants are required to work, but it isn't. Yes, you *should* generate some impressive hours, and you should certainly *appear* to be working extremely hard (see Rule 4).

But your goal should be to do an excellent job on a few files, rather than a mediocre job on lots, because mediocrity is very out of fashion in law firms. Being a reasonable sort of

person you probably think that partners take account of the volume as well as standard of work you're doing, and recognise that there's bound to be a trade-off between the two, right?

Wrong.

Firstly, it's rare that one partner will know what demands are being placed on you by other partners. They all operate in little black boxes, totally isolated from each other (and often the world). It is fatal to assume that they communicate with each other and that they will not make conflicting demands on your time. They don't, and they will.

Secondly, even if they did know what other pressures you were under, they wouldn't care. What they care about is the work you do for them. Each one will expect perfection from you on *his* file, and if he doesn't get it, he will (a) resent it, and (b) remember it.

Thirdly, it is a verity that partners have short memories when it comes to an assistant's contribution to the firm as a whole. Your overall performance may have been stupendous in view of the number of plates you were spinning at one time, but you can be certain that a few years or even a few months down the road, anyone who may once have known the full story will have long since forgotten it.

When partnership evaluation time rolls round, those baggy-eyed months when you foreswore sex and averaged three hours of sleep a night will mysteriously disappear from the collective partnership memory. All they'll remember are the plates that you dropped.

This problem of conflicting demands made on assistants is hardly of recent vintage. Indeed, having been tackled on it over the years by involuntarily departing assistants, partners at most firms are prepared with two facile responses of which you should be aware.

Firstly, they say, assistants are expected to act as 'professionals', i.e. to do top-quality work on everything they undertake. As a practical matter, this is utterly unresponsive to the problem of conflicting demands on an assistant's time. Nevertheless, partners continue to hoist the ill-defined, self-promoting, semi-macho banner of professionalism to support their unrealistic expectations.

The second reply partners give is that assistants should be mature enough to protect themselves. Take them at their word: CYA. Have a bumper volume of the Weekly Law Reports correctly positioned when the boots start flying.

This is easier said than done. The safest approach is to pit the partners against each other, relying on their various levels of seniority to resolve the problem. Thus, when all your available time is being used on a project for Partner Henchley, and junior Partner Auld approaches you for help, your response should be no less obsequious and self-protecting than the following:

AULD: You there! I'd like you to help me draft a prospectus for an offer of convertible debentures that Amalgamated Plasterboard plans to put out next month.

YOU: Uh . . . that certainly sounds like fun. I love drafting prospectuses and have long been fascinated by the particular issues involved in the plaster-

board industry. Can I assume that you have already spoken to Mr Henchley, who said he wanted my full attention devoted to his mother-in-law's will for the next month?

AULD: Henchley, eh? Well, look. Perhaps I can find someone else.

YOU: Oh. Okay. Please let me know if there is any way I can help. I had no plans for this Saturday evening that couldn't be rescheduled for next year.

Note that the only people you can interplead in this manner are partners. Law firms aren't like poker, in which two fives are better than one King. In law, one partner tops four senior assistants.

Rule Three
There is no such thing as a 'Draft'

In legal circles, some words and expressions have become altered through usage. They take on peculiar meanings, remote from popular understanding. They become what are known as 'terms of art'.

One important term of art is the word 'draft'. Failure to understand its specialised meaning has left many an eager and capable assistant consigned to proofreading loan agreements during his (short) stay with the firm.

The potential disaster of misunderstanding the term draft will confront you early in your career. A

REINING IN A PARTNER

A critical skill which every articled clerk and assistant needs to develop is that of preventing the partner with whom they're working from saying something foolish or just plain wrong in front of a client.

Partners tend to bluff a lot in client meetings, and sometimes one of them will go too far. Maybe he doesn't know the area of law as well as he should, or maybe he's just feeling good and gets carried away – anyway, he starts giving advice that you know could send the client into bankruptcy or prison.

Your job in this situation is to stop him. Doing so requires alertness, because you have to see very quickly where the partner is going and cut him off before he reaches the point of no return.

It also requires diplomacy, because you have to interevene without exceeding the limits of your humble station. (You're only there because the partner likes an audience or might want a cup of coffee.)

One approach is to interrupt the partner in mid-sentence: "Mr Peterson, I can see you're about to make another of your typically brilliant ideas, but perhaps we should first explain to Ms. Loram the more conventional approach, so she'll know what her competitors are doing."

If the outrageous proposal is already on the table, you could say: "Another way to achieve the same objective – you were explaining this to me only yesterday Mr Peterson – would be to . ."

Either of these displays of uncommon boldness on your part will probably startle the partner, like a bucket of cold water, into recognizing what he was about to do. At that point he will follow up with: " Oh, yes. Yes, absolutely. We could do that too. Options, Ms Loram – we want you to know all the options."

The partner won't love you for doing this and he definitely won't thank you. But don't let the certainty of his ingratitude stop you helping him out. Remember: whenever a partner is made to look stupid in front of a client, an assistant's head rolls.

partner for whom you've been research-ing an issue asks you to provide her with a 'draft' of a file note on what you've discovered. More often than not she'll camouflage the trap by saying something like "Just do a *quick* draft", or "Just *whip off* a draft", or even "Just *dictate* a *rough* draft". The italicised words should trigger flashing red lights in your mind.

The partner who utters these words does not mean them. When she speaks them, she should be disbelieved. There is no correlation between her expression and her intent.

Notwithstanding how your dic-tionary might define 'draft' ("a first or preliminary writing, subject to revi-sion"), and regardless of the seven years of Latin and three of Greek that you took, and ignoring the two decades you have spent using the language in written and spoken correspondence, this partner wants a *polished, final product.*

That she asked for a draft does not mean she will tolerate typos. That she instructed you to produce a 'rough' working document does not mean you should not double-check all the case references in advance. That she said 'dictate' this piece does not mean she will excuse the absence of captions, headings and footnotes.

Everything you submit to a partner should be suitable for framing. No matter how casual the request, how insignificant the task, or how small the amount of money at issue, the test you should apply to everything bearing your name is its suitability for hanging in the Sistine Chapel (the *newly restored* Sistine Chapel) of le-gal documents.

Note an ironic corollary to the rule that there is no such thing as a draft: *everything must be a draft.*

The point is that while everything you submit to a partner must be your best effort, you should never *admit* that it is your best effort. This is because the partner is bound to change it – not because it needs changing, but because changing things needlessly is what partners do.

For this reason you should put the word 'draft' at the top of everything you submit to a partner, especially things heading ultimately for a client or the court. This conveys two important messages: the first is that it is just a preliminary product, something you could undoubtedly improve upon given a bit more time. the second is that the partner's *invaluable* input will *of course* be necessary to put the document in truly final form.

The first message covers your arse, the second sucks up to the partner – two entirely appropriate messages for someone in your posi-tion to be sending.

The communication problem exemplified by partners' continuous misuse of the word draft occurs in a variety of contexts. Take two other notable examples: *"Just skim the case authority"* and *"take a quick look at the case authority in this area".*

Never should an assistant "skim" anything, and never should an assistant take just a "quick look" at anything. If you miss one case that is even marginally relevant, or one statutory section that is just arguably germane, it will haunt you for years to come.

A last word regarding drafts and other preliminary undertakings: If, in the direst of circumstances, you

"Let's not concern ourselves with partnership, son. A man's reach should exceed his grasp, or what's a Heaven for?"

find yourself unable to complete the exhaustive, perfect work you now know is expected, do not forget Rule 1: CYA.

The best way to do this is to state the limits of your work in a memorandum accompanying what you have produced.

'In the following discussion, I have, as requested, addressed the question of the protection of minority shareholders under S75 of the Companies Act 1980. *I have not addressed the question of directors' duties in connection with such protection.*'

The italicised sentence, although spineless, shifts the burden higher up for any catastrophic problems that occur. It suggests, without saying so, that there was an *understanding* that you would limit your research in the way stated.

Other Misleading Expressions

When a partner misuses the word draft, you can protect yourself – if you have read this book and know what he really means. Often, however, a partner will use a word that signals danger, but there's absolutely nothing you can do about it – nothing, that is, short of throwing up on his desk to cut him short .

In some instances this will prove to have been a moderate response.

These are the phrases to look out for:

"This project will require some creative thinking"

The partner who approaches you with these words is cunning. He is about to present you with a problem that he knows has no solution.

Sometimes a client wants to do something he can't do – like use Lake Windermere as a toxic waste dump. Sometimes a client *doesn't* want to do something the law says he has to do – like tell the Revenue about Aunty Alice's surprise £1,000,000 bequest. Whatever the problem, the partner will come to you for a solution.

It is one of the more craven things a partner will do. He knows there's no solution, because he's thought about it and couldn't come up with one – which is what led him to the remark about creative thinking.

Even if you could come up with a solution, he wouldn't use it, because the chances are there's no authority for it. If there were any authority he'd know.

This partner is covering his arse. He'd rather you were the one who failed to come up with a solution, in case he has to explain it to a more senior partner or the partner who brought in the client.

If he *is* the partner who brought in the client, he's covering his arse anyway – out of habit. After all, that's what got him where he is today.

"Have you ever done any work on [impossibly tedious area of law]?"

The partner who asks you this doesn't care what you answer. If your answer is no, she will say, "Fine, you're about to become the firm's expert on this area." If your answer is yes, she'll say, "Fine, we're going to need your expertise." Her question is almost rhetorical. It is an indirect way of saying you're about to tackle the most mind-numbing area of law known to man. She is justifiably squeamish about telling you this head on, and so tries to disguise it by euphemism.

"Are you busy?"

Your answer to this question should always be an unhesitating "Very busy", even if you happen to be filling in your lottery ticket at the time. Your interrogator is obviously about to ask you to do something – probably something pretty nasty, or he wouldn't have approached you so obliquely. (If the approach is an even more oblique "How are you fixed for time?" you can be sure the job has four legs and barks.)

If you answer merely "Busy", you will be given the job. You may get it even with "Very busy", but you'll at least get credit for carrying a heavy load.

If you're *not* busy and you could do with the hours, your answer should be exactly the same, but with a qualification in language suggestive of your heroic capacity for toil e.g. "Very busy, but perhaps I could *shoulder* some more."

"I'll need about a day's work from you on this file."

This ranks up there with "We value our trainees", "Our property department has never been busier" and "Partnership is guaranteed".

There is no such thing as a one-day project, at least not one they'd bother getting a new person to do.

'One-day projects' usually involve searching for a case or statutory authority that does not exist. The people in charge will have checked the obvious sources already and found nothing. Because your search will turn up nothing either, you'll be required to continue it for days on end, wasting incredible amounts of time as you descend the ladder of obscure sources.

"Familiarise yourself with the law in this area."

The partner who says this doesn't mean you should just find out which statute contains the authority he's looking for. Neither does he mean that you should merely acquaint yourself with the main points of the statute.

He's using 'familiarise' in the way only partners use it: to *master* an area; to know by heart every clause of every statute; to commit to memory every case even vaguely relevant.

It may be that he's just got wind of a deal that's about to happen, or he anticipates a dramatic turn of events in a big case. Whatever he thinks, it'll happen fast, or he wouldn't have given you even the little warning that he did. Moreover, he thinks the area is too complicated to be responsible for it himself. He wants someone else's neck on the line.

Yours.

Rule 4

Cultivate the Image of a Workhorse

In law, appearance is reality. Rule 4 mandates affirmative craftiness and cunning. It exhorts you to be resourceful and creative in your quest for the proper image.

To assist you in this quest, below are some life-saving (and marriage-saving) tips on how to maintain the preferred image while keeping your workload under control. These tips fall into five categories:

Judging your Workload

Let's start with a fundamental truth: billings are important to your career. Even at firms that make a great play of being "full of individuals who value their lives outside the law"*, the partners' greatest lament is that there are only twenty-four hours in an assistant's day. The fact is that, whatever law firm you go to, some level of work is unavoidable. But what level?

The answer to this question depends on your peers at the firm. For appearance's sake, you're going to have to spend roughly as much time working as they do. But only *roughly* as much. This brings us to one of the major tips to ease your burden: do not so much as think about trying to

---

*What these firms are full of is something quite different and much better for plant growth

LOATHSOME CLIENTS – DO YOU
HAVE TO TAKE ON THE WORK?

Occasionally, you will be asked to help represent someone you don't like. It's not just that the work is tedious and boring (that's to be expected), but that you find the client repugnant for ideological or other reasons. Do you have to take the case?

It depends. Are we talking about a situation in which you just don't like the things your client gets up to even though they're perfectly legal? Tobacco companies for instance who instruct you to prepare a defence against an action in tort for nicotine poisoning. If so, the answer is yes, you definitely have to help out on those cases. That's what big firms do. Those kinds of clients are their bread and butter.

But what if it's someone who's done something really awful, something so unspeakably vile that you lose your lunch at the mere thought of the person – Fred West, for instance, or Robert Maxwell. Do you still have to work on the case?

No. But you don't have to remain employed at your firm either. Turning down work is a risky business.

Actually, there *are* ways you can get out of bad projects. But expressing moral scruples isn't one of them. What you've got to do is tell the partner that you're already busy helping some other odious, repulsive slug stay out of jail. Say "Gosh, I'd love to help you on the Noriega case, Mr Owen, but I'm already up to my eyeballs keeping Honecker on the loose."

Whatever you say, don't attempt to explain your true views to the partner in charge of the gruesome work. He knows people scorn him for what he does, and he's hypersensitive to criticism. This is simply no place for candour.

There's a lot of ugly work floating around at the top of the big law firms because the clients who can afford to use their services didn't get rich by being nice folks. If you don't like wearing a black hat, you should consider a different job.

lead the field in billable hours. Not even if the field consists of you and old Mrs Butler in conveyancing.

For one thing, you won't be able to do it. There are always a few super-human grinds around. More to the point, that's not how you want to spend your life. You want more on your tombstone than 'Andrew Palmer, Partner'. You'd like to have at least enough free time to be able to show up for your own divorce.

The only goal you should set for yourself is to avoid the anchor position in your year. That's good enough. For once in your life, as contrary as it is to your nature, be average.

Easy Hours: How to Beef up your Billings Legitimately

Given that you're going to have to chalk up some hours, you should take every possible advantage of the few easy but legitimate ways of beefing up your billings.

Most of your work will not be easy. It might consist of researching safety requirements for off-shore oil rigs, drafting motions for enlargement of time (only a lawyer would attempt to 'enlarge' time), or doing a comparative study of Clean Air Regulations in the UK, France and Sweden.

Such work is boring (you will find yourself filling out time sheets for fun) and extremely tedious. It is like digging ditches in a minefield, which doesn't take much intelligence, isn't glamorous or remotely enjoyable, but you do need to pay close attention to what you're doing.

When something easy comes your way, pounce on it. Of the various ways

to beef up your billable hours, at least three will be available no matter where you work:

Travel

The first and best of these is travel. A shrewd assistant will involve himself in work for continental clients, preferably corporate work that will entail trips to the company's headquarters. The time spent en route to Paris, Milan or Barcelona is billable, and it is a gift from God. Okay, you might have to spend the flight reviewing client papers. On the other hand, you might have to order a double Scotch and watch Rocky 9.

Court Work

The second source of easy hours involves court work of any kind. By the time a case actually reaches court, the solicitor's role is practically over. Your client's barrister takes over and you can sit back and pay only cursory attention to what is going on.

To make your client feel secure (you're there in a sort of hand-holding capacity) and to prevent yourself falling asleep, you should pass little notes to Counsel every now and then. It doesn't really matter what they say, as merely passing them will convince your client that you're on top of the situation.

You should also bring along some blue ruled notebooks. Unless there is someone more junior on your team, you may get the job of noting down every single word uttered in court, but that needn't disturb your reverie: you've had over four years' practice of noting without listening at law school. Those skills are easily recalled.

*"A word of advice, young man. Practise the courage
of your convictions outside the office."*

GETTING AWAY FROM IT ALL

Projects that get you out of the office are not to be taken for granted. Better still are projects which not only get you out of the office, but get you somewhere where it doesn't matter how you're dressed. (Projects where it doesn't matter *if* you're dressed are few and far between.)

Even if this means trekking off to some God-forsaken plot of land to serve an eviction order on 'travellers' who have taken a shine to it, or spending two days in a client's basement rummaging through boxes of VAT records, you will come to relish the opportunity to shed your suit (which hasn't seen a wash in 18 months), your absurd tie (whose only function is to collect tangible memories of your meals) or your uncomfortable tights (which only make it difficult to go to the loo.)

Note: if you're wearing the absurd tie *and* the uncomfortable tights, being stuck in the office isn't your primary problem.

Proofreading

Finally, there are easy hours to be had in proofreading. Every written item that leaves the firm has to be proofread. Partners expect it to be done, and clients grudgingly expect to have to pay for it.

You don't want to find yourself proofreading too often: it looks silly on your CV as your primary field of expertise. Still, it has the virtue of being something you can do at home, stretched out on your sofa, to the melodious accompaniement of Guns & Roses. Also, noticing a few typos that everyone else has missed (a "catch" in legal parlance – as in "Nice catch, Dave. I didn't see that one") can earn big points in the eyes of the partner overseeing the project.

Weekend Work: Avoiding it
and Simulating it

A legal career always involves some weekend work. It was a lawyer who said "Thank God it's Friday. Only two more working days til Monday".

The dilemma is – how much? Legal work is like school work, in that you could always do more in any given area. You could spend every weekend in the office and never run out of things to do.

The goal, of course, is precisely the opposite. In judging how much to do, bear in mind that there are two varieties of weekend work. The first is serious big-time stuff that has been brewing for some time and that has suddenly come to a head. It might be a major complaint to the Monopolies Commission that you've been involved in, the papers are due by Monday morning and you are the only person who can finalise the papers in time.

There is no escape from such work. You should resign yourself to it, exploiting the opportunity to enhance your image as a hard worker. If the partner in charge takes the extraordinary step of *asking* whether you will be able to help out over the weekend, and you know that there is no way out, tell her you'll definitely be coming in.

Moreover, pretend you're glad about it. Tell her you were planning to be in the office anyway. Tell her you *like* weekend work, because it gives you a chance to hunker down without lots of interruptions from the telephones. (Don't worry about the credibility of such an absurd claim. Lots of partners really do like weekends for this very reason).

Above all, do not make her order you to be there. She'll do it, so you won't have gained anything, but she won't like doing it. Once you've started rubbing her conscience the wrong way or convinced her that you're not a team player, you might as well pack your bags and move on.

The second type of weekend work is emergency work: short-term, last-minute, run-of-the-mill stuff that any assistant could do. This type of work you <u>can</u> avoid.

This isn't your emergency; it isn't something they need *you* to handle. In all probability, some partner hasn't bothered taking care of a matter that has been lying around for ages, because he knew there was a stable of assistants he could get to deal with it at the last minute.

Any assistant can deal with these types of emergencies, and you shouldn't be concerned about the propriety of trying to avoid them. What you should be concerned about is how to avoid them. It can be done. (See *Friday Afternoons* opposite)

You might well wonder about the costs of such an approach. Won't people get angry if you consistently manage to avoid weekend work? No they won't because it's unlikely they'll ever know. No one keeps a checklist of weekends worked. Still, it's worth covering your arse here, as everywhere. There are three especially handy devices for doing this.

Firstly, many firms have a receptionist coming in for all or part of each Saturday. This presents you with a great opportunity. Set the alarm for about eleven, call the office, and, using a false voice, have yourself paged. Everyone who is really at the office will assume you are there too, somewhere. That they haven't seen you won't matter: law firms are big places. And don't worry that the receptionist will know you haven't answered your paging call. Lots of people don't as a matter of principle.

Why eleven o'clock? Most people who work on Saturday do so in the morning, so if you call any later you might miss them, as well as the receptionist. On the other hand, the really senior people who come in generally don't do so *before* eleven, so you don't want to call too early.

Besides, it *is* the weekend.

Another way to simulate weekend work is more effective but also more demanding. It requires you to actually go in.

This doesn't have to ruin your plans for the weekend. You don't have to *stay* there. Just go in, look a bit fatigued (not totally knackered – you're supposed to be able to handle the pressure), walk briskly through the library, grab two or three volumes of law reports, return to your office, turn on the lights, and then head for the first tee.

Turning on your lights is vital. The cleaners will have turned them all off on Friday night, so anyone who sees yours burning brightly will assume you've been in.

The joy of this trick is that it keeps working all weekend. In many office buildings, the cleaners won't be round again til Monday evening, so you get the benefit all day Saturday, all day Sunday and even early Monday morning.

Turning your light on after the cleaners have been is a trick capable of application during the week too. If they do their rounds past your office at, say, 7 o'clock, and you happen to finish your game of squash at 7.15, just pop back and turn on your light. It can't hurt your image with the partners who pass by later that night or the few who come in early next day.

If you do come in on a weekend, consider leaving a note on the desk of a partner, just to let him know you were in. You have to be careful here, because it can be a bit transparent. Don't do it *every* weekend, and don't write in red ink at the top of the note "Saturday, 7:00 p.m." Let the partner work out when the note must have been written by, for instance, observing that it was written on the back of that weekend's Church Service sheet. (How you get one of those without having to sit through a 30-minute sermon is another matter.)

The third method of simulating

FRIDAY AFTERNOONS
THE ART OF LAYING LOW

Friday afternoon is a critical time. It's the time when partners start checking their diaries to see what needs to be filed in Court on Monday morning. It's the time when your weekend stands the greatest chance of being destroyed.

Try to avoid answering your phone after Friday midday. On no account should you check with your secretary for lunchtime messages. Once you've been told that a partner is looking for you, you're caught. (After the way you've treated your secretary, she certainly cannot be trusted to hide the fact that you don't return your Friday afternoon calls.)

Avoid walking past partners' offices on the way to the lavatory. If possible, don't even *go* to the lavatory on Friday afternoons. If you absolutely have to, find a nice end-of-row cubicle and stay there the rest of the day.

Ideally, you should arrange to be out of the office altogether. An appointment with your dentist will do. If that isn't possible, the next best strategy is to set up camp in a corner of the library. Take your books and files and whatever you're working on with you – the bigger the pile you surround yourself with, the better. You want to give an impression of utter immovability.

Make sure it's an *obscure* corner of the library. It's not unusual for partners to prowl around on Friday afternoons in search of hapless assistants for weekend duty. Also, you want to be able to ignore your name when it goes out over the paging system. If you're in a crowded area, some idiot will tap you on the shoulder to say he thinks he just heard you being called.

What about matters that *have* to be dealt with on Friday afternoons, come what may? Use the library phone to arrange your restaurant booking and weekend tennis game. Everything else can wait.

weekend work requires you to brown-nose the porter on reception. With flattery and a quarter of Teachers, you should be able to persuade him to sign your name on the check-in list that a lot of law firms maintain on weekends.

All those who actually come in will see your name as they sign their own. Even better, they *won't* see a mark beside your name indicating that you've left – clear evidence that you've outlasted them all.

The only danger with this trick is that others may be doing the same thing. If fifteen assistants' names appear in alphabetical order in identical handwriting, someone will smell a rat.

UNDERSTANDING BILLABLE HOURS

When lawyers talk about billable hours, they usually refer to annual figures. Below is a chart that breaks down the annual figures into weekly figures and then puts them into perspective. In evaluating these figures, bear in mind that billable hours don't (or *shouldn't*) include time you spend eating lunch, arranging a game of squash, or discussing last week's episode of Baywatch. An accepted rule of thumb is that forty billable hours requires sixty hours in the office (except in some City practices where you start billing as soon as you wake up).

Annual	Weekly	Interpretation
4,000	80	Wrong profession; junior doctor.
3,500	70	Pathological liar.
3,000	60	Barely conceivable, and then only if living with camp bed in office.
2,500	50	Sweatshop hours. Brutal but possible, given lots of travel. Probably guilty of substantial padding.
2,000	40	Very respectable in most practices.
1,500	30	Civilised lifestyle, assuming no heavy non-billable duties.
1,000	20	An assistant with this number could only survive if he calls the Senior Partner 'Dad'.
500	10	Sole practitioner (Tiverton).
25	5	Dead (but no one has realised yet).

All-Nighters

All-night work has a lot in common with weekend work. It's unpleasant and should be minimised, but it gives you a chance to extend your image as a hard worker.

Like death, all-nighters cannot be avoided indefinitely. When your number comes up, remember two points: (1) Do it gracefully; and (2) don't keep it a secret.

The first point is crucial. Because everyone has to do an all-nighter at some time, no one is going to feel sorry for you. If you whine about it, you won't even get credit for your dedication, because everyone will know you did it grudgingly.

The preferred posture is one of ease and nonchalance. This suggests that you are possessed of unusual stamina. (Let your colleagues think that you wouldn't *ever* go to bed but for social reasons.)

It also suggests that you do this sort of thing all the time, which carries the further implication that other, more senior lawyers view you as the person to call upon in a crisis – the can-do guy. Over time it will have partners and assistants alike believing that you get called in for the *hard* cases.

The only problem is that your 007-like insouciance under pressure will be wasted if no one knows about it. Hence the second point: Don't keep your all-nighter a secret.

In practice this point can conflict with the goal of handling the all-nighter gracefully. Talking about it all the time is inconsistent with shrugging it off as commonplace. You should therefore make considerable efforts not to do all-nighters solo. With someone else present, word of your energy and stamina will spread.

If you can't arrange company, don't despair. You can make your exertions known to the partner in charge of the case by showing up in his office next day wearing the same clothes as the day before.

When doing this, make sure your clothes are orderly (shirt tucked in, belt buckled, bra facing forwards), because you don't want to look out of control. However, your shirt should be wrinkled, and your beard shadow suitably dark (particularly impressive on women) – these things you couldn't be expected to do anything about.

Another reason you shouldn't be too distressed by a lack of company for your all-nighter is that when you are alone you can take naps on the conference room sofa. Before lying down, however, take the precaution of arranging for a trusted friend to ring the conference room extension early next morning. It's professionally embarrassing to be caught bashing out Zs when you're supposed to be polishing up a flotation document.

General Image Tips

Keep your secretary busy. This is especially important if you share her with a partner. The partner will gauge your productivity from the amount of work you give your secretary.

Not that any of it will actually get done. The secretary will use the partner's work as a pretext for avoiding yours so she can finish the latest issue of Cosmo. She isn't there to

"Randolph here has just finished his first all-nighter.
Brings back some great memories, doesn't it?"

work eight hours a day – at least not for some lowlife assistant.

Nevertheless, you must make the effort. One way to give the impression that you are keeping your secretary busy is to keep her in-tray loaded with papers. What kind of papers doesn't matter. If you need one letter typed up, attach it to two or three large files and leave the whole stack in her box. The partner will see the stack and be impressed.

Another way to generate a large volume of material for your secretary's in-tray is to use a separate cassette for each letter you dictate. In a single hour on Monday morning, you can produce enough tapes to suggest a whole weekend of work.

Some particularly important image tips relate to those occasions when you want to knock off a little early – say, around lunchtime. This will occur once in a while. Hey, you've got a life to lead. But CYA.

Firstly, always leave by the stairs rather than the lift. Even if you're on the tenth floor. A partner who sees you heading for the ground floor in a lift will be suspicious, no matter how full your briefcase or how purposeful your expression. On the stairs you can speed up or slow your pace to avoid meeting anybody else and, *in extremis*, you can always duck into the lavatories next to the stairwell.

Secondly, prepare for any telephone calls that might come in after

LAVATORY ETIQUETTE

Partners don't like seeing assistants in the lavatory. It means they aren't in their offices racking up the hours. Your objective should be to meet partners in there so rarely that they start looking for the outline of your colostomy bag under your suit jacket.

Never follow a partner into the lavatory. If you go in, and see one already there, do a sharp about-turn and leave. If you're already installed in a cubicle when a partner comes in, take the precaution of lifting your legs off the ground so that your shoes and trouser bottoms are no longer visible from the other side of the cubicle door. Some partners have developed the skill of identifying work-shy assistants just by the pattern of their soles. Wait until he goes into a cubicle himself and, as far as you can tell, has committed himself to being there. Then make your escape.

If you're standing at the urinal when a partner comes in, simply close up shop and leave. This is no great hardship. Most assistants can't function with a partner nearby anyway. (If the partner occupies the urinal right next to you, even though there are ten empty ones in the room, you face an entirely different set of issues.)

It is a truism of big-firm life that entering the lavatory causes you to be immediately paged. Conspiracy theorists allege that the lavatory seats are equipped with heat-seaking sensing devices and that each assistant's buttocks are individually coded into the system. Partners at firms we spoke to would neither confirm nor deny this allegation.

If you're determined to take something to read with you, make it a letter or something that will fit into your pocket. Don't stop at reception, tuck the Times under your arm, and head on in. So brazen a declaration of your plans for the next fifteen minutes is crass in the extreme.

The combination of stress, coffee, egg & bacon sarnies, and legal documents gives the average lawyer the natural gas output of New Zealand. Releasing this in your office mysteriously summons your secretary. Unlike your university colleagues, she will not think this hilarious. Neither will you when the work stops getting done.

you've gone. You don't want your secretary telling partners that she doesn't know where you are, but she saw you leaving at midday carrying your golf clubs and wearing Ray Bans. Partners take a dim view of assistants who work a half-day (or a quarter-day, as it would be for some City firms).

Tell your secretary or the receptionist – whoever takes your calls in your absence – that you're off to a meeting (you don't need to say *which* meeting.) Say you'll be back when it's finished, but it might not end til after the office closes. The point you want to convey is that although she might not see you again til tomorrow, she should tell callers that you've gone "out", not "home".

If you're worried that a partner who gets this message might work late that night and wonder why he didn't see you around, call in for messages after nine holes. Otherwise just be prepared to say that, because of where the meeting was held, it made more sense to stay there to finish reviewing "the papers" (there are always papers) than to return to the office.

What about partners who pass your office in the early evening and see no signs of life? Make sure there *are* signs of life.

Your light should be on, of course. That's basic. But go the extra mile. Leave a jacket in plain view, preferably on the back of your chair. Shrewd assistants keep a spare jacket in the office specifically for this purpose. (Make sure it's the *jacket*, you leave rather than trousers. The implications are entirely different.)

Also, leave a full cup of coffee on your desk. Lawyers make a lot of money, but most of them are as tight as a camel's arsehole in a sandstorm. They just can't believe someone would waste a *whole* cup of coffee.

In your quest for the image of a workhorse, keep in mind that you can score big points by being in the right place at the right time. If the firm has a partnership meeting at 7.30 a.m. on the first Wednesday of every month, find some excuse for strolling by the meeting room at 7.25 a.m. with your sleeves rolled up and your hair *not* bearing that 'just-got-out-of-bed' look.

The same principle applies on days when the weather or Jimmy Knapp has brought the public transport system to a halt. Half the secretaries will call in swearing that their cars won't start. You might be tempted to do the same. But in these situations you have a tremendous opportunity to amass Brownie points.

Set your alarm for what will seem like the middle of the night, and make an all-out effort to get to the office by seven. Invariably, one or two partners will have done the same thing, motivated by white-collar machismo to be able to tell their friends the strike didn't keep *them* from the office.

When they see you there early, they will recognise you as "their kind of guy". They won't commend you – you're only doing what's expected – but they'll remember it and always think better of you than your workshy colleagues who weakened when the going got tough.

A good example of the kind of dedication you should simulate was provided by the bombing of St. Mary's Axe in April 1992 which blew out three hundred windows of Norton

Signs of Life

1. *Light burning brightly.*

2. *Suit jacket on back of chair.*

3. *Uncapped pen.*

4. *Full cup of coffee. (Make sure it's full; half-cups are common.)*

5. *Perma-glow cigarette.*

6. *Half-eaten sandwich.*

7. *Phone with blinking 'hold' button.*

8. *Open Weekly Law Reports.*

9. *Shoes. (How far could you have gone without your shoes?)*

10. *Open briefcase. (Keep a spare around for this purpose. You should be carrying your first one when you leave the office.)*

11. *Open filing cabinet. (Partners would never believe you'd leave it open all night.)*

12. *Legal pad with writing cut off in mid-paragraph, or even mid-sen*

Rose's offices. According to a spokes-man "One partner was thrown right across his office by the force of the blast. He went straight back to his desk and carried on working." Mad? No, just an ambitious lawyer going about his everyday business..

A final tip on cultivating the proper image: never leave your office without a volume of law reports, or pad of legal paper tucked under your arm. Over the years, partners will subconsciously come to associate you with the implements of labour. That association will help carry you where you want to go.

Rule 5

Avoid Peripheral Involvement in Anything

Every now and then, you will be called on to perform a small task in connection with a big case. The partner in charge will assure you that your time commitment will be minimal and that your end of the work will be both interesting and educational.

Use any excuse to avoid this task. It can only bring misery.

Your work will not be interesting. No case is so interesting that it cannot be broken down into boring constituent pieces, and the premise of your involve-ment is that you will be working on one of the most subordinate pieces.

Nor will your work be educational.

No one will explain the background of the case to you or bother to keep you informed of its progress. You will work in an absolute void – not dis-similar from what your social life has become since you joined the firm.

That the work will be boring and educationally worthless is the least of your problems. *Lots* of your work will be boring and educationally worthless. The main problem is the enormous potential for damage to your reputation. Once you have done anything on a case, people expect you to know everything there is to know about it, and they'll think you're a complete imbecile if you don't have its details at your fingertips.

They forget the tangential nature of your involvement and become irri-tated by your lack of comprehension. The fact that you don't know what is going on is not mitigated in their eyes by the fact that no one has *told* you what is going on.

To add insult to injury, you will forever after be on called on for emer-gencies requiring weekend work and all-nighters in connection with the case. In big cases, emergencies occur all the time, and an asssistant who has done as little as fifteen minutes of work on such a case is deemed to have special responsibilities with respect to its most onerous tasks.

The problem of peripheral in-volvement is not unlike that of becoming familiar with an objectionable area of law. Once you have so much as glimpsed the Industrial Waste (River Protection) Act you are forever deemed to be the firm's expert on the subject.

The lesson? Where possible avoid any cases that strike you as odious, regardless of how minimal your

"Thank you, Mr Rogers, for those amazingly astute comments on the margins of my memo."

involvement is likely to be. And remember: your willingness to play the role of the courteous dinner guest, cheerfully consuming whatever slop is put in front of you, will only bring you second, third and fourth helpings of the same.

Rule 6
Give Partners What they Want

Lawyers like to think of themselves as scholars. It's the way they explain to themselves why they don't earn as much as commodity dealers.

But if you want to succeed in a large firm, shed all pretensions of scholarship. Practising law is a trade. Whatever you learned in law school, a lawyer is like a garage mechanic, except that the lawyer charges more because his toolbox is made of leather and called a "briefcase".

What partners want from you when they ask for a summary of some point of law is something they can insert wholesale into an opinion letter. This doesn't mean your product should be clear and readable. You *are* a lawyer. But it should not be an article for publication in a Blackwell's periodical. If you produce a think-piece, or an academic treatise, they'll make you do it again.

No doubt this will frustrate you. Throughout law school the tutors emphasised the scholarly aspects of law. You learned that pursuing an argument to its impossible but logical conclusion is where it's at.

Ignore all that. Satisfying clients is what the partners are trying to do. Satisfying partners is what you're trying to do.

Rule 7

Stay alert to your Long-term Prospects.

If you are content at your law firm and doing well, you might as well stick around. On the other hand, if you expect to leave the firm, whether voluntarily or with a size ten brogue footprint on your derriere, you should know that a junior assistant enjoys greater mobility than a senior one.

Law firms prefer legal virgins, so to speak. They think that a lawyer who has spent more than two years elsewhere has lost something vital.

It's also a question of inter-firm competition and pride. Firms are hypersensitive to the suggestion that they might be willing to take on an assistant who didn't cut the mustard elsewhere. Some of the most prestigious firms are the most insecure in this respect, snubbing "used"

assistants like so much dental floss.

It is also the case that a young assistant has greater credibility than one who is, say, five years qualified, when he claims that the first firm just didn't live up to his expectations – that it didn't, for example, have enough work to keep him busy past eight or nine o'clock at night ("and I just couldn't stay at a place where they work part-time".)

Law firm recruiters reinforce the theory of immobility between firms by telling you that you'll never have a second chance to join their firm if you don't join them now. "Turn us down now" they'll imply, "and that's it."

In reality the doors to the Church are always open. Okay, perhaps not *always* open, or not at *every* church. And you might have to give up a year or so in seniority in transition, but you're certainly not trapped for life.

Remember, it's a lot easier to switch firms than switch spouses – and people do both all the time.

If the problem at a given firm is that *you* don't like *it*, you needn't worry too much about how it regards you. You don't want to make such a hash of things that they padlock your office and give a pack of Dobermans a whiff of your handkerchief. But basically, you are the one that decides when to walk.

If, on the other hand, you are happy where you are and could imagine still being there five or ten years down the road, you need to keep a look-out for the various indicia of your progress compared to your peers.

There is really only one indicium that matters, although it travels under many names: bread, dosh, dough, spondulinks, wodge, wad. Some have even been heard to call it "money". You will hear stories of other indicia, such as interesting work, travel, nice office space, or a secretary willing to correct typos. Firms themselves will tell you that your annual performance appraisal is the best way of telling how you're doing, although no assistant in his right mind believes that (except in negative circumstances where, for instance, the evaluating partner demands your office key and asks where you would like your post forwarded to.)

But if money isn't everything, it is definitely way ahead of whatever comes second. If you fall behind the rest of your year in salary, you would be well advised to start buffing up your CV.

The Star System

Law firms operate on a star system. By the time of qualification, a few assistants will already have been identified as the stars of their year. There's no awards ceremony, but everyone knows who they are.

Being singled out as a star is a self-fulfilling prophecy. Stars receive the best work (such as it is) and the most responsibility – in short, the greatest opportunities to shine.

You don't get to be a star by caring about the outside world. If you've already been designated a star, you aren't reading this book. The big question is, what if you're not one of the stars of your year. Do

"What do you think you're doing, Saunders? Just killing time?"

you bail out? Work three times as hard? Sabotage the stars?

If you're sure that being a star is what you really want, hang in there. The fact that you're not a star yet doesn't mean that all the vacancies are permanently filled. Circumstances can cause a star's lustre to fade.

On *Not* Making Partner

Even with the help of this book, there's a chance you won't make partner. Most assistants don't. Times are hard for law firms these days, and partners are looking for reasons *not* to let you on board, rather than the reverse.

Make no mistake: doing excellent work is no guarantee of partnership. Often the partners just don't feel like dividing the cake any further. And why should they? *Lots* of assistants do excellent work. The legal profession is blessed and cursed with a surplus of talent.

The bottom line is that partnership decisions reflect the Screwee Rule: they'll do it to you if they can. The only assistants they can't afford to screw are those who have developed their own clients – Young Rainmakers – or who have carved out indispensable areas of expertise.

The prognosis for the middle-ranking assistant who is neither a rainmaker nor specialist is grim. A survey by Legal Business magazine in 1993 reported that morale within the profession is at rock bottom. One unhappy assistant told the magazine, "The partners in this firm appear not to know about the abolition of slavery." Another commented that he and his peers felt like a generation betrayed – a generation that was lured by false promises of success but now lives in fear of unemployment.

It's widely thought that regional firms are an easy touch compared to London firms – that is, you can have good quality work *and* quality of life and as long as you're not completely half-baked you're bound to make partner. Alas, this dream combo is yet another illusion. You may get two out of three, but never all three, as made very clear in a Times profile of Dibb Lupton's managing partner, Paul Rhodes:

> 'He sits at his desk, monitoring fee income from around the country on his computer. With a stab of his finger, he can tell how much one of his employees is billing to the minute. Fall short, and he will be on the phone, screaming down the line, striking fear in the hearts of secretaries and partners alike.'

The provinces don't welcome charity cases from the City.

If you do get shot down, in London or the provinces, ask yourself if life would have been so marvellous even if you'd made it. Are those really the people you wanted to spend the rest of your life with? Not making partner could be compared to getting bounced out of a leper colony. The world outside may be better than the one you're leaving.

SIGNS THAT YOU'RE ON THE WAY OUT

How can you tell when things aren't going well for you, that the partners consider you an 'also-ran', that you're on your way out?

The subtlest of bad tidings is being fed poor quality work. Instead of growing less boring and tedious over the years, your files continue to extend new semantic reach to those two adjectives. However, given that all assistant work is boring and tedious, it can be hard to discern a trend one way or the other. (It's like asking whether French lorry drivers are more objectionable than French farmers – it's just impossible to say.)

A somewhat clearer sign is being 'frozen out' altogether: new work just isn't sent your way. At first this seems like a blessing – you're exhilarated to have your evenings free, and you revel in being able to spend ten minutes in the sunshine at lunch. Then you realise your learning curve is plummeting, you find it difficult to get into three figures on your weekly time-sheet, and you begin to dread going into the office because of the whispers that accompany your every step.

Take heart. Don't sit in doubt, wondering when the axe is going to fall. Watch out for the signs below, and you'll be able to predict with complete accuracy the moment of truth.

➤ Your new office has no desk, no window, and a seat that flushes.

➤ The librarian asks for collateral each time you take out a book.

➤ Your annual salary rise is in four figures – including the ones to the right of the decimal point.

➤ Your secretary is replaced by a typewriter and a copy of "The *Kogan Page Guide to Model CVs*'.

➤ The firm formally considers you for partnerhsip every three months, just so they can tell you you've been passed over *again*.

➤ You're given work from people junior to yourself – including the post room.

➤ Your client contact is restricted to clients whose wills have become effective.

. . . and the consequences

What exactly happens if you don't make partner? You die, usually in poverty, always in disgrace. Most spurned assistants leave their firm within weeks, others last a few months – long enough anyway to see their spouse commence divorce proceedings.

The most common cause of death is starvation, although a surprising percentage are able to overcome the immobilising effects of depression sufficiently to take their own lives.

A few find positions delivering take-away pizzas, but they too lose the will to live once the other moped riders find out what happened and begin mocking them.

In any event death seems merciful after a few weeks of the indignities that befall passed-over assistants. Some of the least of these indignities are:

1. Your children come home from school every day with bloody noses and bruises, after fighting with other children chanting "Oliver's father wasn't made a *paaartnerr*."

2. Your children stop coming home from school with bloody noses and bruises because they've begun claiming they were adopted.

3. Strange dogs approach you and pee on your leg.

4. Strange people approach you and pee on your leg.

5. You pee on your own leg.

"Do you hear me, I was partnership material."

TWELVE SURE-FIRE WAYS TO END A LEGAL CAREER

➤ When one of the Partners announces that his wife is pregnant, distribute a memo denying reponsibility.

➤ On the morning of a big court case, tell the partner in charge that it's a shame the Embassy World Snooker final was such a cliffhanger last night, because you would have liked to have time to check your case authority properly.

➤ Come in to the office at the crack of noon – two days in a row.

➤ Tell a client how the time he's been billed for was really spent.

➤ Send polemical letters to The Times on the firm's notepaper and signed in the firm's name.

➤ At the Christmas party, get drunk and vomit on the Senior Partner's wife

➤ Voice your opinion that internal procedures described in John Grisham's 'The Firm' bear an uncanny resemblance to those of your own firm.

➤ Score with a secretary that a partner has been stalking for months.

➤ After a game of squash one lunchtime, hang your jockstrap or bra (or both) on a conference room door handle to dry.

➤ Suggest that conflicts of interest preclude your firm from acting for Unilever.

➤ Fail to read this book.

➤ Write this book

CHAPTER EIGHT

ONCE YOU'RE A PARTNER

'The Crock at the End of the Rainbow'

The mere thought of partnership mesmerises some assistants. They daydream about it, drooling like basset hounds remembering old marrow bones. According to assistant myth, partnership is a blissful state, synonymous with heaven, paradise, and other realms free of famine, disease, war, and proofreading.

If you subscribe to this view, stop and think for a moment. Ask yourself why partners continue to leave their office lights on when they go home at night. Who are they trying to impress?

Ask yourself why they still make a big show of reading documents while they're standing at the urinals; why you never see a partner idling round the coffee machine chatting about last night's telly with the secretaries. Whose approval are they trying to cultivate?

Is something amiss in paradise?

Whether partnership will even approach your fantasies depends on a number of factors, most importantly the size of the firm you're at.

The most obvious difference between large and small firms is size. Hence the labels "large" and "small". But the differences don't stop there. Read on.

The Small Firm

At a small firm, making partner might bring only a marginal improvement to your working life. Consider four key criteria:

Grunt Work

At small firms, staffing is, by definition, lean. This means there are limits on how much grunt work you can avoid. Okay, you won't have to do as much as before, but you'll have to do *some* – more than enough to

"Welcome aboard, Sanderson. You're one of us now."

keep you from forgetting, when all is said and done, that you're still practising the same law you did as an assistant.

Money

Small firms aren't supported by a proletariat of assistants generating three times as much in client fees as they're paid. You don't get a gush of money to the pyramid's apex the way you do in large firms.

This means that unless you're a recognised specialist with enough clout to play ball with the big-league

firms, the only yacht you'll be sailing when you make partner at a small firm is the one with the rubber band motor that you still play with in the bath.

Job Security

Job security in the law depends on having big commercial clients who need regular legal advice, year in, year out. In a recession, they're the ones that keep you afloat, and in a boom they are a *fantastic* gravy train. The problem for small firms is that big companies feel more comfortable with big law firms advising them. This is frustrating for small firms. Kevin Dink in the Mile End Road may be every bit the litigator that Sir George Campbell of Broadgate Towers is, but if he pitches for BP's account the only thing he'll win marks for is chutzpah.

The other disadvantage small firms face is the constant and calamitous possibility of a partnership split. What do you do if your sole expert on the one-bite rule leaves to set up his own dog-law boutique?

Prestige

How great can the prestige at a small firm be? You can't impress people at drinks parties, because it's unlikely that anybody will have heard of your firm, and if they have, its because your offices are right on the High Street sandwiched between Martin the Newsagents and the Light of India takeaway, which says it all.

Other lawyers will arrogantly assume that you're at a small firm because you couldn't make the grade at a big one.

None of this necessarily matters. What do you care about prestige? Your friends like you because you're nice to children and you feed stray cats. People of the opposite sex like you because you can part your hair with your tongue. What more do you want?

The Big Firm

At a big firm, partnership is very different. Not necessarily better, but different.

Prestige

If your firm is big enough, strangers will have heard of it. They might not be impressed, especially if its letterhead has all the exclusivity of an anti-poll tax petition and your name appears near the bottom. But they will have heard of it.

Another reason they might not be impressed is that they will understand what you had to sacrifice to become a partner at that firm. More importantly, they will understand the limited nature of the benefits there. Why limited? Because an essential fact of life in the big firms today is: *Partnership ain't what it used to be.*

Job Security

Until not so long ago partnership meant a job for life and a guaranteed share of the firm's profits. That is no longer true. Less productive partners at the big firms are being forced to retire early or just plain fired. It used to be understood that the whole point of working like a slave – the phrase at big firms is "work like an assistant" – was to be able, eventually, to slow down. No longer.

Life at a big firm isn't like a village egg-and-spoon race, with separate prizes for each age group, good-spirited slaps on the back for the fallers, and everyone getting together afterwards for a few beers. It's more like an Olympic marathon, where there's only one division – the all or nothing division – and if you can't keep up with the youngest and the fastest, you're out.

Note, however, that there's one key difference between the big-firm race and the Olympic marathon: in the big-firm race, there's no finish line. You run flat-out till you drop*.

Autonomy

Well, you say, at least there's the autonomy, the control of your own destiny – partnership at a big firm guarantees that.

You're kidding, right?

It's the very nature of partnership that everything is subject to vote. Therefore, you *are* vulnerable to being removed, and the partnership can, if it has the collective will, control every aspect of your working life from how much holiday you take to what colour carpet you have in your office. If they decide to move against you, your individual vote will be about as effective a defence as stuffing a hankie down your trousers seconds before Devon Malcolm begins his run-up.

"You know, Dickins, the law still surges through every inch of my being."

You can't take on a new client, or even a new matter for an old client, without checking with everyone else that there are no conflicts with existing work. For that matter, the other partners can veto your new client if they don't like his looks or his politics – or his lawyer.

Is it part of your game plan to reach sixty and still have to simulate hard work when what you really feel like is a quiet kip at your desk?

Money

At one time a partner's pay was based largely – or even solely – on seniority. Other things being equal, more seniority meant more pay.

Today you might find yourself getting *less* money with each passing year, rather than more. It just depends on how the partnership wants to divide the cake.

Couldn't you increase your share somewhat by working a little harder in a given year? Aside from the fact that you're probably already working harder than the human cardiovascular system can bear, it's up to the partnerhsip – which might or might not choose to reward your additional labour.

The money that comes with partnership at a big firm is likely to be substantial. But put it into per-

*A 1991 survey revealed that 7.7% of all solicitors who died that year were between 35 and 44. That national average is 1.7%

PRACTICAL SKILLS THEY OUGHT TO OFFER
VETERAN LAWYERS — *BUT DON'T*

• Not talking about law on social occasions.

• Resisting the call of nature during contract negotiations.

• Making bills look reasonable.

• Pretending the assistants who work for you may make partner one day.

• Persuading rich people you're a fantastic lawyer.

• Persuading friends and relatives you're a hopeless lawyer.

• Sucking up to secretaries and other support staff.

• Pretending you respect your partners.

• Pretending you trust your partners.

• Pretending you like your partners.

• Pretending you like your partners' spouses.

• Pretending you've never fooled around with your partners' spouses.

• Reconciling the demands of work and getting divorced.

• Retiring before you're pushed out by your partners.

spective: there are 26 year old dealers in the City making £200,000 a year, and innumerable bankers making twice that.

And, perhaps more relevant, the money that a just-made-up partner makes isn't a great deal more than what a senior assistant makes, which suggests that there's nothing instrinsically magical on the other side of the partnership line.

"Did you see the new regulations on partnership capital accounts? Quite fascinating, I must say."

"We got round S27 by transferring stock to Stein's dog and letting it take the short-swing profits."

"The question is – what effect does an eclipse of the sun have on 'market overt' doctrine."

Tax Lawyer

Passionless eyes. Hates small talk. Would have become an actuary if he'd had more personality. Motto: "The Code is Lord"

Corporate Lawyer

Young partner at City mega-firm. Promises that one of these days he's going to meet his two year-old son. Motto: "Sleep is dispensable"

Academic Lawyer

Jurisprudence is where it's at. Turned on by statute books. Has lectured in same jacket for 6 years. Motto: "Anything to get published"

"About your sister's cottage. We don't normally do residential work, of course, but in this case . . ."

"So I said to Jagger, 'Mick, baby, never sign anything without running it by me first.'"

"Maybe my client shot a few people, maybe he didn't. But there's a principle at issue here."

Property Lawyer

No. 1 recession-victim, struggling to fill time-sheet. Lives in terror of partnership announcements. Motto: "Don't expect me to go quietly."

Music Lawyer

Pop star manqué. Basks in reflected glory of clients, denying the banality of what he does for them. Motto: "I can relate"

Litigation Lawyer

Hired gun and proud of it. Even trivial cases consume a forest of giant redwoods in document copying. Motto: "Concede nothing"

CHAPTER NINE

ELEMENTS OF STYLE:
THE LAWYERLY LOOK

*'A wardrobe as dull
as your work'*

There are various points of style every lawyer should observe. For assistants these points can gain you critical mileage in the minds of the vast majority of partners who will never see your work and who know you only socially (or antisocially, as the case may be). For partners, the idea is essentially the same. There is always someone more senior you need to impress.

Arguably, it doesn't matter much how lawyers look. After all, they spend most of their time in their offices, and when they do get out it's usually just to see their counterparts at other firms. Still, unless you've already given up hope for a better life, it's worth paying some attention to how you look.

MEN

Conservatism should be your watchword. This doesn't mean you

have to be stuffy. Your suits can run the whole gamut from blue to black, with occasional pinstripes for a festive touch. Single-breasted suits are preferred, and shoulder pads should be avoided at all costs. Partners like their lawyers to look like lawyers, not Larry King.

Shirts should be plain coloured or in narrow single-colour stripes. You might favour alternating cerise and yellow stripes half an inch wide, or think that Indonesian batik is really you, but partners view flamboyance with deep suspicion.

If you have a hairy chest, the office is not the place to sport it. Make sure your shirt is 'Oxford' cotton rather than ultra-fine Egyptian. The rug may work wonders in Cowes Week, but it looks terrible poking out between your shirt buttons. This is especially true of women.

Shirt collars should never be button-down. Partners distrust anything that smacks of foreign dress codes. They think a Brooks Brothers shirt is just the start of an inevitable slide down the formality scale, and that if they don't nip it in the bud, their assistants will turn up for work wearing funny loafers with tassles on them, and using McEnroe-like negotiation techniques. (*"Delete clause 17? You want WHAT! You cannot be serious! You guys are the PITS!"*)

Ties should be narrower than the prevailing standard, whatever it is. Silk, not nylon, and if they have to have a motif, preferably something a little more sophisticated than that of your University Honking club. Stripes and spots are fine, but don't get cute with one of those trompe d'oueil numbers. Apart from the fact that they look like dead fish hanging down your shirt, they are often 'hand painted' which throws into doubt their ability to hold beer, coffee and saliva stains without smudging.

Accessories, like clothes, should be confined to the plain and practical. If you've always dreamed of wearing a Mont Blanc Meisterstuck in your breast pocket, carrying your papers around in a Louis Vuitton wallet, and whipping out your Psion to do some spreadsheet analysis, you're in the wrong game. Most lawyers are completely brand-ignorant and strictly utilitarian in their choice of products, and any unnecessary ornament is frowned upon.

Wear a simple watch: you really don't need one that tells you the time in Adelaide, nor one of those heavy diving numbers that Connery wore in *The Hunt for Red October*.

It is worth keeping *one* decent pen on you, however, for that rare occasion when a partner turns to you for something with which to sign a document. You don't want to have to fish through your trouser pockets only to come up with a tooth-marred Bic with lint balls caught in the clip.

The Exception: Lefty Chic

'Man at Mansfield' deports himself in an entirely different plumage from that described above. The uniform is less strict and has as its centrepiece an item as symbolically fixed as it is contextually flexible – the black polo neck. Whether at work, in a BBC studio, or on a street demo, the black polo neck never looks out of place and never looks in need of a wash. Truly, once subsidiary rights are sorted out with the Milk Tray man, its radical credentials will be supreme.

WOMEN

Except at the stuffiest London firms (which is to say, the stuffiest firms in the world), it is now okay for women to wear dresses rather than suits. This represents progress. Until not so long ago, women in the law felt compelled to look like men. Now they just feel compelled to *act* like men.

Otherwise, the rules of drabness are the same. Your attire should match the job. Make-up should be minimised and perfume avoided altogether. You don't want to encourage the Senior Partner to think of you in the same vein as the women he knew in Paris during the War.

Hemlines should stay at or below the knees (or partners' eyes won't).

ARE YOU A REAL LAWYER?

A law degree and success in Finals do not a *real* lawyer make. There's more to being a real lawyer – such as messing up sentences by reversing the subject and predicate (see above). How can you tell if you're a Real Lawyer, an *Arnie* of a lawyer? Measure yourself by the following criteria:

➢ **Real Lawyers eat fast food.** The faster, the better and preferably something they can eat at their desk. Eating just gets in the way of work.

➢ **Real Lawyers don't have tans.** They prefer the library to the beach. It's not easy drafting a prospectus while lying in the sand.

➢ **Real Lawyers don't drive flashy cars.** Rainmakers might, but nobody said they're real lawyers. Real lawyers aren't into style or ostentation.

➢ **Real Lawyers don't have beards.** Not even the men. Beards are bushy and untidy. Even a moustache looks too much like nose hairs out of control.

➢ **Real Lawyers don't have erotic daydreams.** They don't have trouble concentrating on their work. For a real lawyer, tax reports are erotic enough to hold their attention.

➢ **Real Lawyers love to proofread – everything.** Not just legal documents and formal correspondence. Real lawyers proofread street signs, food labels, menus, even the lists of personalised number plates that appear in Saturday's Daily Mail. Nothing makes their day like catching a typo.

➢ **Real Lawyers don't like children.** Children are noisy, frivolous, distracting. They just don't care about the important things in life – Mem & Arts, Directors' Liability, the Yellow Book etc.

➢ **Real lawyers like fact, not fiction.** Too often novels depend for their storyline on coincidental events, and lawyers just can't accept that. They can't see the point. They like hard information, untainted by the intrusion of an author's imagination.

Avoid dresses with slits up the sides unless (a) you have great legs, and (b) you're bucking for promotion to receptionist.

Your hairstyle should be inconspicuous, preferably gathered up in a wad at the back. Anything too stylish will give the impression that you spend a lot of time fussing with it when you should be working.

Shoe heels should be low, if not flat. High heels will just cause you to be confused with secretaries.

Large breasts should be avoided. Partners will stare.

The Briefcase

Carry a large expandable black one. No *business* person would be caught dead carrying such a monster – someone else handles their grunt work – but lawyers *thrive* on grunt work. They take pride in walking out of their offices on Friday night with two of these briefcases, each big enough to hold a human body.

You should do the same. It's all part of cultivating the right image. You needn't actually have anything in your case, although some file documents are handy just in case you find yourself sitting next to a partner on the train in the morning. Pulling out a copy of *Viz* just won't do.

CHAPTER TEN

OTHER
LEGAL CAREERS

(1) Civil Service Lawyers
(2) Country Practice

Private practice in an urban law factory isn't the only route. Some of the finest lawyers around opt for legal work in the civil service or head for the hills.

The Civil Service Lawyer

The primary advantage of being a lawyer in the civil service is early hands-on responsibility. You get none of these two-year warm-up periods before getting to argue some piddling motion for extension of time which is standard private practice training.

A civil service salary is nothing to write home about compared to what some lawyers make in private practice. And you shouldn't be too worried about your creature comforts. Civil service lawyers required to travel are sometimes surprised to discover that there's a class lower than 2nd on British Rail – and it's no fun at all if you're allergic to animals.

But if you measure income in pounds *per hour*, it's far from clear who comes out on top. If private firms spawned the concept of the 25-hour working day, government lawyers spawned the concept of the 25-hour working week.

Being a civil service lawyer just might be right for you – no private firm has a bigger client – but don't make any rash decisions. Read the following rules on survival as a civil service lawyer, and be sure you know what you're letting yourself in for:

• Insist on having your own desk

Nothing is certain in the civil service. It is too much to hope for a private office, but demand your own desk. In fact, negotiate this before you accept the job.

• Brush up your secretarial skills

If you got through law school without learning how to type, now is the time to learn. The good news is that word processors are not beyond the competence of even technopeasants like yourself. The bad news is, there's a reason they're so simple. Read on:

There are a number of perfectly good secretaries working in the civil service (people debate whether the number is two or three), but you will not get one right away – say, within your first ten years. You will get another kind, to whom filing fingernails is more important than filing papers.

Do not be too harsh in judging these secretaries. They work under trying conditions. Handling five lawyers' work output between the hours of ten and three-thirty with an hour and a half for lunch takes some going. In judging them, consider how your own performance would suffer if you wore a Sony Walkman all day.

Secretarial self-reliance is essential to government practice. You don't have to be able to take apart and reassemble a Xerox copier, but it wouldn't hurt. You will invariably be the next person to use a machine after someone has dropped a box of paper clips into its guts. (When the lights start blinking, do not panic. Just leave the room quietly and find another machine.)

• Dress Functionally

Dress is not as important in the civil service as it is in private practice. A government salary can't support a Bond Street wardrobe, and let's face it, who wants to wear a £600 suit behind a £50 IKEA desk.

• Avoid Drift

The pace of the civil service can be pleasantly slow, to say the least. You will undoubtedly be tempted, on a prolonged basis, to relax, settle back, borrow your secretary's Walkman, and give no thought to the future.

Resist this temptation. You're there to learn and advance, not drift. The civil service has a thousand dead ends – somebody has to draft those regulations governing the composition of sausage meat – and you don't want to find yourself stranded.

Don't assume it will be obvious when your career has come to a halt. Unlike the private sector, the civil service doesn't operate on an up-or-out system. You might be doing the same thing in thirty years that you did when you began. (If you have any doubts about what this will do to your mental agility, try having a conversation with the 'lifer' at the end of the hall.)

At a minimum, learn skills that are transferrable to the private sector, e.g. litigation skills. Reviewing documents under the Offical Secrets Act might be exciting for two days, maybe three, but a year of it could turn you into a civil service lawyer forever.

The Crown Prosecution Service

The CPS is traditionally regarded as a dumping ground for lawyers who couldn't cut the mustard in private practice. Whatever the truth of that prejudice, the CPS is not a happy ship. Those entering in the last few years have seen their prospects for advancement blighted by modernising reforms of the service – objectively no bad thing, but cold comfort to those who joined the CPS because it was advertised as a safe option with a steady well-defined career structure.

The Seriously Flawed Office

If the CPS is feeling a bit duffed up, the SFO is on the ropes and about to hit the canvas. Despite respectable conviction rates in its smaller fraud cases, its score in high profile cases is positively Norwegian. Blue Arrow, Roger Levitt, George Walker, Guiness II, III and IV – the failures trip off the tongue with a fluency that belies the millions of pounds of public money poured into them. At the time of writing, it looks as if the 'successful' Guinness 1 prosecutions may be quashed too on the grounds that the SFO withheld evidence.

There are several theories about why the SFO has been so ineffective in the big cases. One that doesn't hold water is that it lacks resources. Guinness I to IV cost the taxpayer £27 million.

The more likely reason is, from the SFO's point of view, less palatable. It is that the lawyers, accountants and policemen who populate its corridors just aren't up to the job. They keep on screwing up. The professionals and policemen within the SFO are said to get on like matter and anti-matter. The Big Bang, when it happens, is likely to be painful for both groups.

And it might happen very soon. The word on the street is that the SFO may be merged with the Fraud Unit of the CPS. This will save money but send morale plummeting even further. As one CPS staffer put it, "we need the SFO like a hole in the head."

Talk about creative tension.

> Country Practice

The joy of being a country lawyer is that you're as much a feature of country life as the postman, the newsagent, the old folk sitting on the village bench, and the ramraiders from the council estate. You're part of the fabric of the community.

The *problem* with being a country lawyer is that you're also part psychologist, part family therapist, and maybe part plumber and animal midwife. You're part of the fabric of the community. This means Morris Dancing on Saturday mornings at best, and being cast as the back legs of the panto donkey at worst.

Depending on your tastes, the balance may be a positive one. Whatever country pursuits you're press-ganged into, who's to say it's worse than being told to perform anatomically impossible acts on yourself on the London Underground each morning. (If the mugger is armed, you may find the acts aren't impossible.)

The major difference between the city lawyer and country lawyer is the level of perfection that goes into each job. City lawyers always attempt a perfect job, no matter how disproportionate the costs are to the stakes involved. They'll not only produce a fifty-page lease for a tiny industrial unit, but also spend thousands of pounds of their client's money proofreading it.

Country lawyers don't do this because their clients can't afford it. They have to do something City lawyers *never* have to do: pull in the reins, perform cost-benefit analysis, exercise some *judgement.*

CHAPTER ELEVEN

WOMEN IN THE LAW

'Subpoena Envy?'

You don't have to wear briefs to work on them. The gender ratio of entrants to law school is now about 50:50, and the same for people going on to do training contracts.

But what about where the real money is – at the partnership level in the big firms? Here too, we see a degree of change: no longer do the greybeards talk fearfully of "those funny chaps who wear lipstick and dance backwards". At least not openly. And the ratio of women to men being made up as partners is improving every year. But the fact remains that men still vastly out-number women at the head of the notepaper.

For those of you discouraged by the distance that remains between the reality and the ideal, there may be some comfort in knowing that male lawyers are not nearly as chauvinistic as, say, scaffolders, cattle ranchers or ayatollahs. You won't find your en-trance to the conference room being greeted by lecherous wolf whistles or suggestive remarks. This is due not only to the enlightening (not to say emasculating) experiences of law school, but also to the brutal hours most lawyers put in. As with prisoners of war, their carnal urges take a backseat to the demands of sleep and food. In certain City firms, Cindy Crawford could walk the corridors without raising an eyebrow.

Interestingly, a few lawyers re-spond in the opposite way, becoming sexually omnivorous, playing on any-one and everyone in the indiscriminate manner of sharks munching on the dangling legs of passengers from a just-capsized cruise liner.*

---

* Occasionally they get their come-uppance: Last year a mar-ried partner at a City firm sent an E-Mail message to another partner's secretary inviting her to a lunchtime sex romp. Her E-Mail response – "Alright, if you don't mind my hairy legs round your neck" – appeared on every screen in the office when he hit the wrong key on his computer.

*"So you went to law school, and now you want to
practise law. I think that's sweet."*

But even these legal lechers don't match other industry standards, for the simple reason that lawyers are less likely to persist in the face of rejection. They know only too well the possibility of a sex-discrimination lawsuit. Also, as veterans of social rejection – most lawyers have been encountering it since they were toddlers – they know better than to hope to overcome it.

True, a few old codgers still find the time and energy to nurture their fear of female competition. 'Traditional'attitudes tend to linger, like dog do that gets into the crevices of your trainers and won't come out no matter how many times you rub them on the grass or scrub them with the washing-up brush, and you end up having to leave them outside so they don't pong up the house.

Faced with such attitudes, women can adopt one of three responses:

The Crusader

A kind of scorched-earth approach, this involves addressing every single offence or inequity, without regard to size or context. The main problem is that it requires so much energy. It's a noble battle, but exhausting.

The Mata Hari

Some women, motivated by frustration or contempt (or both), undertake to exploit those feminine resources that male partners appear most willing to recognise and reward. You can spot a hard-core Mata Hari by her black mesh stockings and garter belt.

The Survivor

This pragamatic approach consists of equal parts diplomacy, thick skin and sense of humour.

> "Certainly, I'll get you some coffee, Mr. Hart – if you'll pick up some tampons for me when you go to lunch."

It involves not letting your core values feel threatened in situations that require you to endure a conversation about, for instance, whether Jimmy White should have gone for the blue in the side pocket, or played safe with the long green. Who knows – you may even like croquet.

Whichever attitude you adopt, take comfort in two things: firstly, even bigots find it impossible to sustain the myth of male superiority when confronted with the evident failure of the male-run criminal justice system over the last thirty years.

Secondly, women not only make up over half of all new entrants to the profession, but they are getting into, and excelling at, the top law firms. They represent an increasingly high proportion of the partners made up each year, and not just in the 'soft' branches of the law. As they continue their inexorable advance into every area of the profession (proving slowly but surely that they can be every bit as dull and compulsive as men) and as they ascend to control of the *client* companies, their success in the law will be consolidated.

INTERNAL AFFAIRS

The traditional taboo on intra-office intimacies – "Don't dip your pen in the company inkwell" – has been expressed in a number of different ways, always from a male viewpoint. Most notable is the "hamburger rule", which advises against getting your meat at the same place you get your bread.

Every firm has at least one lecherous partner and more often than not, this person is male. Lecherous female partners are not common features of the legal landscape – the profession is not so advanced. This lecher may or may not be single. He may or may not be attractive. He is, invariably, smooth and confident. He will sit down in your office, cross his legs, and straighten his tie in a slick way that says here, at last, is a guy who really knows how to sit down, cross his legs, and straighten his tie.

What you should realise, if you find yourself attracted by his act, is that you won't be sharing it; you'll be adorning it. Another notch on his bedpost. He may come on subtly: "Amazing, your eyes are the same blue as my Ferrari." Or he may be more direct: "How about lunch on Sunday. Come round early . . . say, Saturday night." However the liaison begins, it won't last. Afterwards, you'll just be another source of office smirks.

Don't even imagine that having a fling with a partner will advance your career. Certainly, *he* may become an ally in your fight for advancement (though even that is doubtful), but you'll make enemies of all the other partners, who will be green to the gills that one of their colleagues is having more fun than they are.

As far as "horizontal integration" is concerned (i.e. assistants getting friendly with other assistants) the dangers are fewer. Your motives are not suspect, because the alliance cannot enhance your competitive position.

The major problem in going out with another assistant is, of course, what happens after you break up. Unless your firm is gigantic, you will still bump into each other on a regular basis. You will have to suffer in silence when he or she turns up at the Christmas party with a new companion. (Groin kicks are considered unprofessional except in certain Leeds firms.)

Perhaps the best policy with respect to intra-office affairs is to apply a 'rebuttable presumption against' i.e. it is presumed that the costs will always outweigh the benefits, but the presumption may be rebutted in exceptional cases. For women, such special cases have been called the 'Kevin Costner Exception'. For men, the 'Victoria Principal Principle'. In these cases, the costs of an affair *can't*

Female solicitors in City law firms know only too well that if they become pregnant their chances of partnership instantly vaporise. The prudent course is to postpone having children until after you have been made partner. One female partner confided to the OLH that the day she made partner she stopped taking the pill.

"We didn't rush into hiring our token female because, quite frankly, we wanted to be damn certain it wasn't just a fad."

In the course of researching this book, the publishers were anonymously sent an old internal memo from one of the major City firms. We publish it here, despite the threat of proceedings, to give you some idea of the way the profession used to be.

<u>MEMORANDUM</u>

To: <u>All Partners</u>

Re: <u>Ladies in the Profession</u>

Partners will have noticed that ladies have been entering the profession in droves over the past five years. Apparently they just don't care what happens to their children, or who does the ironing — but that's emancipation for you.

Anyway, at a firm of our size, we need to show a certain sensitivity to these matters, and you might find the following tips of use:

1   Avoid the term "girl lawyer". It seems to cause offence (perhaps because, deep down, the kind of ladies who enter the profession wish they were chaps.)

2.   Don't ask a lady lawyer to get you coffee or tea. Ask her to ask your *secretary* to get it. It wastes time, but seems to make them feel better.

3.   If you ever say "damn" or "blast" in front of a lady lawyer, apologise immediately and let her know you don't expect her to be able to handle such rough language.

4.   When you're involved in a firm social event, don't hide it from the ladies. Let them know, and emphasise the extent to which firm matters were discussed so they know their interests were considered and they feel involved.

5.   Most lady lawyers are happiest doing matrimonial or trust work but if you want to use one for litigation, use a plain one, so that if you come up before a lady

judge, you won't be disadvantaged (obviously, no lady judge is going to rule in favour of someone slimmer and prettier than herself).

6. When speaking to a lady judge, use the standard "Your Honour" form of address, as in "Is it Your Honour's time of the month?"

7. This respectful attitude should be maintained at appellate level. For example "The Court below was clearly approaching *its* time of the month." Or even — to demonstrate your sensitivity to the problem of sexist language — "The trial judge was clearly approaching *his* or *her* time of the month."

8. If you're involved in a jury trial and a lady lawyer expresses an interest in working on the case, take the time to explain that women simply aren't competitive enough for this sort of work, that the softness and innate passivity that makes them so charming renders them unsuited to the rough mood of the courtroom. There may be tears, but in the end they know it makes sense.

9. Many lady lawyers harbour romantic feelings towards partners — who amongst us has not, at one time or another, been the subject of a painfully obvious 'crush' on the part of one of our young articled clerks? It is tempting indeed to let matters progress, especially as any ensuing entertainment is tax-deductible. To avoid the appearance of sexual favouritism, however, you should first have her fired. This may seem drastic, asking you to go to all that trouble just to avoid the appearance of impropriety, but such are the burdens of membership of this fraternity which we call the law.

D.B.L.   14.6.92

CHAPTER TWELVE

LEGAL WRITING

"Excuse me, but what does this say in English?"

Everyone knows that legal writing is different from normal writing. People can understand normal writing.

Legal writing is unintelligible but instantly recognisable. There's no mistaking a "whereas" or a "forthwith". You can spot a "hereinafter referred to as" miles away. (Talk about floccinaucinihilipilification!) Why do lawyers write like this?

Several reasons.

Firstly, they like big words. Lots of people like big words, but dealing with them ten to twelve hours a day affects your brain, altering your perspective on what is sesquipedalian and what isn't.

A lawyer will say "vehicle" when he means "car", and he'll say "practicable" when he means "practical". (No one outside the law has even heard of the word "practicable".)

The second trait that makes lawyers write so peculiarly is that they are exceedingly meticulous by

nature. This translates not only into aberrant eating habits* but also into an unnatural fear of ambiguity and a craving for precision in their prose.

Take the following sentence from papers relating to a charge of living off immoral earnings:

> "Instead of running an hotel on the premises, the Defendant decided to set up a brothel, which is the subject of the present proceedings."

---

* Watch how some corporate and all tax lawyers eat each vegetable on their plate in strict succession before moving on to the meat, and finally the sauce, rather than moving back and forth between them as most people do. Spooky!

This sentence would distress most lawyers because of the pronoun "which" in the fourth line. The average lawyer would be worried about its ambiguity: does "which" refer to the brothel? To the Defendant? Or to the morality of his operation?

The mere hint of a possibility of confusion would torture the lawyer's conscience. The same obsession with order that led him to colour-code his notes in law school would lead him to rewrite the sentence as follows:

> "Instead of running an hotel on the premises, the Defendant decided to set up a brothel, which brothel is the subject of the present proceedings."

The additional word adds nothing but length to the sentence. It distracts the reader by its unnatural placement.

But a lawyer would always say *which brothel* just as he would always say *which contract, which court,* or *which* anything else he could think of. The extra word satisfies his infancy-based urge to keep things neat and tidy. With it, he'll sleep soundly tonight, gurgling and cooing, at peace with the world.

The third trait that accounts for lawyers' bizarre writing style is their innate conservatism. The average lawyer is not bold by nature. His ambition is to go through life without unforeseen incident. To this end he qualifies everything he writes, instinctively fearful of being caught in an exaggeration or even a metaphor.

Stylistic peculiarities are most evident in the way partners edit anything produced by trainee lawyers or assistants. Every partner thinks he's a bit of a wordsmith. To be invited to edit Stroud's Dictionary of Judicial Words and Phrases would be the greatest accolade imaginable. There is no sentence so straightforward that he will not happily torture it beyond recognition. Take the simple sentence **"the sky is blue."**

Puh-lease!

No first year trainee would be so naive as to think this proposition could pass muster in a big firm. If she made it through law school, she knows enough to say "the sky is *generally* blue."

Better still, "the sky generally *appears* blue." For extra syllables "the sky generally appears *to be* blue."

A senior assistant seeing this sentence might take pity on the trainee and suggest that before showing it to her partner, she should put it in a more 'lawyerly' form. At the very least, the sentence should be revised to say "*In some parts of the world,* the sky generally appears to be blue."

Armed with these qualifiers, the trainee thinks herself protected. Her conversation with her partner will proceed thus:

PARTNER: You say here that in some parts of the world what is thought of as the sky generally appears to be blue. I assume this is an early draft. Could I see the final version?

TRAINEE: Uh, that's all I've done so far . . . what exactly do you mean?

PARTNER: Well, it's a bit bald, isn't it? I mean, just to come out and assert it as fact.

"SPEAKING AS A LAWYER..."

Lawyers often preface their remarks with "Speaking as a lawyer.." Is this a boast? A disclaimer? Whatever it is, it's unnecessary. It's obvious when someone is "speaking as a lawyer." For one thing, lawyers over-enunciate their words, smacking their lips and pronouncing each syllable crisply and distinctly, as if talking to someone for whom English isn't a mother tongue. This can be irritating. Sometimes it makes you want to insert their tongues into the office shredder.

Lawyers also talk in uncommonly full, formal sentences. They take pains to select just the right words for their thoughts, with mid-sentence pauses so long you could squeeze in a quick reading of *War and Peace* in the interval. It's as if they're talking on the record – for posterity.

A lot posterity cares.

TRAINEE: I'm sorry? Are we talking about the same thing?

PARTNER: Well, this business about the sky – what do you mean by the sky?

TRAINEE: Well, I mean what I see when I look up . . . at least when I'm outside. Isn't that what everybody sees?

PARTNER: Well, if you *mean* only when you're outside, you should say so. Ashursts would love to rip us apart on that kind of mistake. And what about at night? Even at night? I see stars at night – are *they* blue? Do you mean everything *but* stars, or do you mean when there are no stars out?

TRAINEE: I suppose I mean in the day.

PARTNER HURST: You *suppose?* Susan, this isn't a game. We can't go around supposing things. Besides, what about the sun? If it's daytime, the sun will be out, or do you know something I don't?

TRAINEE: Well, of course . . . I mean, no, I don't, but no one in their right mind stares at the sun. They'd go blind.

PARTNER: What support do you have for this comment about "some parts of the world"? *Which* parts? Does it have to be stated so broadly? Can't we say "In London" or wherever we mean?

TRAINEE: That sounds fine to me. I just never thought anyone would challenge such a basic proposi—

PARTNER: And what do you mean by "generally thought of"? Thought of by whom exactly? Lawyers? Scientists? Pigeons? For goodness sake, Stephanie, this has more holes in it than Swiss cheese. I haven't seen such sloppiness in all my years at Cower, Cringe &Tremble. Take it away and come up with something better thought out.'

PRINCIPLES OF LEGAL WRITING

➤ Never use one word where ten will do.

➤ Never use a small word where a big one will do suffice.

➤ Never use a simple statement where it appears that one of substantially greater complexity will achieve similar goals.

➤ Never use plain English where Latin, *mutatis mutandis*, will do.

➤ Qualify virtually everything.

➤ Do not be embarrassed about repeating yourself.

➤ Do not be embarrassed about repeating yourself.

➤ Worry about the difference between "which" and "that".

➤ Never refer to one's opponent's "arguments" – he makes "assertions", and they are always "bold".

➤ If a lay person can read a document from beginning to end without falling asleep, it needs work.

Even more startling for new trainees than this distortion of English by verbally incontinent old-timers is the process by which a legal 'case' is assembled.

Law students are taught that judges decide cases on the basis of (a) statute, and (b) existing authority. As far as case authority is concerned, the system is supposedly ruled by precedent. Accordingly, students assume that the way lawyers construct their argument is by researching previous cases and applying the present facts to them.

What really happens is that solicitors, in collusion with the barristers they have instructed, write the arguments *first*. They know what they want to say; they know how their argument has to turn out.

The file is then passed to a trainee or barrister's pupil, with each assertion followed by a bracketed note

'Find case support for this statement.' This process obviously assumes that there *is* case support out there for any statement.

There is.

If you ever get charged with this stunningly demoralising task, make sure you don't overlook one of these references. For some reason, judges get upset when they find remarks in the case documentation like *'Cite the usual crap'*.

What about those few propositions so obscure or implausible that no authority can be found for them – even by the army of assistants which big firms readily commit to the task? You can't just abandon them. You take a deep breath, put them up front and call them 'self-evident'.

"Edkins, find me authority for the proposition that the law is an ass."

CHAPTER THIRTEEN

DRAFTING LEGAL DOCUMENTS

'More is better – unless it begins to make sense'

Lawyers like to think there's something special about the way they "draft" legal documents. The word itself suggests refined skills, even artistic capabilities. They know that any dwork can, in time, learn to write letters weighed down with legal mumbo-jumbo, but to draft a really good lease agreement you've got to have the sort of warped genius of a Rubik Cube champion.

Drafting truly impenetrable documents is not easy. Many young lawyers' have their first few attempts rejected outright by partners who offer helpful comments like: "This won't do at all Flynn. I can still get the gist of some of the sentences."

Fortunately, most documents have been drafted hundreds, even thousands of times before. Firms keep precedents of the most common ones on computer, and have heaving shelves full of every other conceivable kind. An assistant who is asked to produce a lease for a client's new office block just has to rummage through the precedents and tell the support staff the code number of the one he wants printed off. Then he fills in the blanks.

Let's face it , a trainee in his first week could do it. Trainees in their first week *do* do it.

Sole practitioners don't usually have such extensive or well-organised precedent banks, but that doesn't mean they have it any harder. There are numerous books for sale with model contracts, leases, and wills of every imaginable sort.

If your client is a Hindu who wants to leave all his possessions to his sacred cow, the precedent books will have several versions of the form you need. Just fill in the name and address of the cow.

TYPES OF LEGAL DOCUMENTS

There are only four types of legal documents:

1. Boring
2. Extremely boring
3. Comatose
4. Pull-the-plug-and-let-me-die-with-dignity

There are four types of lawyers producing these documents:

1. Boring
2. Extremely boring
3. Comatose
4. Those for whom the plug has been pulled

The last are easy to spot. They're the ones with all the dignity.

Notwithstanding this simplicity, legal documents come in a dazzling array. Whether you need something to finalise the terms of a deal or, more importantly, to put under the short leg of your desk, you have an impressive smorgasbord to choose from.

In part this reflects the complexity of modern transactions, in part lawyers' zeal for their trade. It also reflects the rabbit-like creative powers of legal documents. Left alone in a drawer at night, leases beget sub-leases, wills beget trusts, deeds beget mortgages, debentures beget subordinate convertibles – with a fecundity of biblical proportions.

Thus far, the only known form of birth control is a client who refuses to pay his legal bill – which reveals in yet another context the merit of learning to "just say no."

How to Draft a Contract from Scratch

Drafting requires most skill on those rare occasions when a client wants to do something that's never been done before. In such circumstances, you can't just rehash an old precedent. You have to obfuscate on your own. Here's how to go about it:

➤ Describe what it is your client wants to do in normal language.

➤ Lengthen it.
Begin the lengthening process by making express provision for every conceivable turn of events, no matter how remote. Be sure to stipulate which party is at risk if an outbreak of malaria among Indonesian cane harvesters jeopardises the market for vintage Aston Martins, particularly if the contract deals with office space in Birmingham.

➤ Lengthen it again.
Define the obvious and qualify the irrelevant. Don't hesitate to define things in improbable ways. A good lawyer has no problem defining 'person' as "corporations, partnerships and livestock"; 'car' as "aeroplanes, balloons and bicycles"; and 'cash' as "stocks, bonds and whisky."

➤ Don't be satisfied with your useless definitions and qualifications. Go through it again and again, expanding clauses and inserting redundancies. This will enable you to avoid the perils of clarity inherent in certain forms of punctuation like the full stop.

➤ Once you've revised your original description to the point where no one without a Phd in semantics will know what's going on, the next step is to break it down into numerous paragraphs, sub-paragraphs and sub-sub-paragraphs. This way, the various units can refer back and forth to each other – "as provided hereinabove in subsection 43(d) except for sub-sub-section (viii) thereof" – thus eliminating any hint of continuity or readability.

By the time you've completed these steps, your contract should defy analysis by GCHQ cryptologists. All that remains is to add a few exhibits, attachments, and appendices. These don't have to be relevant to anything. They're for bulk – roughage for your legal digestive tract. The pinnacle of the art is to have an attachment to an exhibit to an appendix, with cross-references to documents not even included.

A Word of Warning

Opposing lawyers never sit down and draft a contract together. One side takes first crack at it, the other studies it, then they thrash out a compromise.

If you're not the lawyer who did the first draft, remember that the most dangerous part is not what is *in* it but what's *not in* it. An import/export agreement which fails to state that English law should prevail could have you arguing your client's breach of contract case in Bulgaria. An artificial insemination agreement that doesn't say what happens if your client's bull proves choosy about his dates could have you testing your powers of advocacy before a tribunal of farmers in a barn (possibly a Bulgarian barn).

DRAFTING AND PUNCTUATION:
THE PERILS OF FULL STOPS

A full stop marks the end of a sentence. This is clearly understood. That's why they should be avoided. Commas, too, tend to clarify rather than obfuscate, and they are discouraged for the same reason.

God only knows the proper use of a colon. And a semicolon is only half of that. Their indeterminacy makes them valuable tools from your point of view, giving you the power to extend sentences almost indefinitely. With liberal and utterly random use, subjects can be separated from objects by as many sides of diarrhetic text as you care to insert between them.

Dashes and brackets too, if properly employed, can generate a nicely convoluted sentence. Brackets within brackets, in particular, can demand endless checking-up and re-reads.

But far more important than anything you say in a document is whether you are consistent in your use of letters, numbers and Roman numerals. The same lawyers who view a readable contract as beneath contempt become distraught if they come across a bungled cross-reference, forward or backward.

Revising documents is therefore fraught with danger. If you eliminate or, more likely, add a single clause or paragraph early on, all subsequent numbers and letters are thrown out of kilter. That is why you see so many amendments and addenda at the *end* of documents. Lawyers are terrified of making a hash of the numbers.

Two related points : (1) The initial draft produced by your opposing lawyer will usually be quite reasonable, provided nothing goes wrong; and (2) something always goes wrong.

If you're lucky things will go so badly wrong that the contract will prove irrelevant – where, for instance, one side goes bust, or both sides breach the contract in a thousand different ways, or both sides realise that the litigation would go on so long that only their grandchildren will be around to hear the Court's decision.

In these kinds of situation you may get off the hook even if you let your opposing lawyer's incredibly one-sided first draft through. In most situations, however, the wording of the contract is critical, down to the last dotted 'i' and crossed 't'. Your obligation is to make sure it has everything it should have – or you may leave the firm without everything *you* should have.

Legal Machismo

Lawyers like to say that words are their stock in trade. If so, they are burdened by an excess of inventory. Why are they so enamoured of length in their documents? Partly, no doubt, because most lawyers are men, and men have always been enamoured of length – a phenomenon traceable to the feelings of inadequacy experienced by every young boy as he contemplates the superior weaponry of his father as Oedipal competitor. But that's for another book.

There's a touch of Hemingway in all of us, but lawyers can't run with the bulls or go deep-sea fishing, so they find surrogate manhood in their papers. They deny the desk-bound tameness of their lives by thinking of their documents as weapons of battle. A lawyer refers to a contract of which he's particularly proud as "bullet-proof", meaning it can hold up under even the closest judicial scrutiny. Hostile takeovers are full of talk about "Poison Pills", "White Knights" and "Mexican Stand-Offs". The objective is to "wipe out" your opponents or "blow them out of the water".

This white-collar machismo finds its most comical expression in the pride lawyers take in the length of their documents. A lawyer boasts of a hundred page contract the way a sportsman boasts of a hundred pound fish. He'll show it to his family and friends like a little boy showing off a hole he's dug in his back garden. The difference is that the fish and the hole didn't cost thousands of pounds. And if you thought about it long enough, you could find something socially useful to do with the fish and the hole.

AMONG v BETWEEN

A lawyer who doesn't know the difference between "among" and "between" would be better off in a more productive sector of the economy – say, professional kick-boxing.

Until you have time to delve into this difficult but fascinating area on your own, you may be able to get by with the following rule of thumb: when the parties to a contract number three or more, the contract should recite that it is entered "by and *among*" the parties. When there are fewer than three (usually two), the contract should recite that it is entered "by and *between*" the parties.

Why it is not enough simply to say that the contract is entered "by" the parties is an issue going to the very heart of the law.

The Myth of the Reasonable Contract

Contracts are not neutral documents. Lawyers draft them *for* their clients, and their terms favour the client of the lawyer who drafted them.

A lease by a landlord's lawyer, for example, will provide for penalties if the tenant doesn't pay his rent on time, and capital punishment if it happens twice.

The same lease drafted by the tenant's lawyer will give the tenant a thirty-day grace period for late rent, and provide for written apologies by the tenant if he doesn't pay by then.

So one-sided are most documents that lawyers keep two versions of each type of document in their files –

one version drafted for one side, one version for the other. In contract negotiations, they sit around bitching about the outrageous provisions in the other side's proposals, knowing full well that they would be arguing exactly the same provisions if roles were reversed. Concessions are made and eventually, after numerous chargeable hours have been expended, the two sides agree on a 'reasonable' compromise.

The joy of this process is that it enables each side's lawyer to give the appearance of driving a hard bargain. The truth is that they know from the very beginning of negotiations which points they are prepared to concede and which the other side will concede, and could finalise terms inside one cup of coffee if it suited them.

"I tell you, Galworthy, it's the height of the art . . . . a document composed entirely of fine print and disclaimers."

CHAPTER FOURTEEN

LAWYERS AND HUMOUR

'There are no funny lawyers – only funny people who made a career mistake'

When corporate lawyers claim that their work is beneficial to society as a whole, it makes you wonder who's writing their material. These are funny guys!

Lawyers are not known for their scintillating wit however and are generally perceived as humourless, sober and drab. This perception is not entirely their fault. It is due in part to the nature of the matters on which they are consulted. You don't go to a lawyer for a periodic check-up, the way you do to a car mechanic or gynecologist (who, by the way, should be two different people). You go to a lawyer for a divorce, a personal injury claim, a tax problem – things that seldom put a smile on your face.

Besides, lawyers at the end of a week are totally exhausted and ready to do a face-down in their dinner. You can hardly blame them for not setting the world alight.

The fact that lawyers are not the *source* of much laughter doesn't mean they can't enjoy a good joke told by someone else. Lawyers laugh long and hard at jokes told by judges, wealthy clients and Inland Revenue Inspectors. They may not *know* many jokes, but they are able to *appreciate* jokes.

Given the comical nature of what they do (and all of what they bill) it is surprising that more professional comedians do not emerge from the ranks of assistant lawyers. Charging £180 per hour for proofreading breeds an acute sense of the absurd.

The most peculiar aspect of humour in the life of assistants is the extent to which they must confine it to other assistants. Partners who have been known to laugh out loud at jokes told by other partners show a marked reluctance to acknowledge humour out of the mouths of assistants.

This behaviour could reflect a

When judges joke, lawyers laugh.

conscious effort to impress young lawyers with the seriousness of the firm's work. It could also reflect partners' revulsion at the thought of how assistants spend their time – not an unreasonable response.

More likely, however, is that it reflects a psychological defence mechanism. Partners don't want to grow too familiar with people who they may well have to turn down for partnership at some point in the future. This phenomenon resembles the reluctance of jailers in Ancient Rome to become over-friendly with prisoners about to face the lions.

LEGAL GRAFFITI

There once was a lawyer named Rex

Whose thing was too small to have sex.

When charged with exposure;

His plea on disclosure was

"De minimis non curat lex."

CHAPTER FIFTEEN

THE COURTS

*'Old litigators never die –
they just lose their appeal'*

Litigators are proceduralists. They care less about who gets beheaded than whether the guillotine was well-oiled and running true on the day.

Suppose a litigator is told that his client, a handyman at the BBC, has just been charged with assault after rushing onto a chat show and pouring a bucket of water over one of the guests, say, Jane Seymour.

His reaction would be quite different from a normal person's. He wouldn't say "My God, Steve, that's fantastic! What a hero!"

Instead, he would go over the facts with a fine-tooth comb, and look for an angle on which to base his case. "Does Bob read that mag she's always in? If so, we could argue diminished responsibility" or "If she was talking about her book on romance, there's a case for provocation – check the tapes."

Obviously, these questions have only a tenuous connection with justice and fairness. But to the litigator they're an essential part of the system.

What system? The so-called 'adversary system', which rests on the premise that out of the clash of lies, truth will emerge.

The basic problem with this system is that neither party has an interest in reaching a fair result. They both play for *all* the marbles, not just a share, and in so doing obscure as much of the truth as possible.

The litigator's role in this system is to help his client obscure and obstruct. In *discovery*, for example, where each side has the right to ask the other for information relating to the case, does either lawyer turn to his client and say "Give him the papers, John. We have nothing to hide"?

Of course not. The lawyers procrastinate for months, ultimately either holding back the one relevant document, or providing it at the last possible moment hidden in a train-load of irrelevant file-fodder.

Both sides' lawyers then go back and forth to the court filing Motions to

"Speed it up Mr Holman. They tried a case like this on L.A. Law in half an hour."

Compel Disclosure. This process takes eons, and generates gigantic legal fees.

The amazing thing is that litigators are unembarrassed by this role. They like it. When they describe themselves as "hired guns" they do so with *pride*.

To say the least, a litigator shouldn't be someone who is easily embarrassed or who reflects a lot about the end result of his life's labours. But a lot of young lawyers get sucked into litigation departments because that's just about all law school taught them to do. Sadly, a number of perfectly nice people, quite capable of being embarrassed, end up as litigators.

> HAVE I GOT A
> COURT FOR YOU . . .

The High Court divides itself into a number of specialised courts that dispense factory line, bulk-process justice. Some of the main ones are described on the right.

➡

Probate Courts

These courts resolve disputes over the property of dead people. If someone dies owning enough money for a round trip taxi ride to the Probate Court, people will fight over it.

Landlord & Tenant Courts

These courts decide whether a landlord *really* has to provide heat and hot water, and whether a tenant *really* has to pay his rent. These conflicts tend to evoke judges' latent class-based political sentiments. Hence tenants should be wary of judges wearing MCC ties and landlords should be wary of judges with beards.

Juvenile Courts

As Aunt Rose used to say, "people do the strangest things". Some of them break windows, steal cars and stick sharp objects into people they don't know. Juvenile Courts decide whether these high-spirited youngsters should lose their pocket money for a whole week, or whether (if psychiatric reports show that Mummy was a bit careless with the nappy pin) less severe discipline will suffice.

LITIGATION POSTURING

Litigation is a form of low theatre. Pre-trial and in the trial itself, solicitors and barristers are constantly posturing and bluffing, putting on emotions which as lawyers they are quite incapable of feeling but which

are calculated to enlist the support of the judge.

Occasionally lawyers on opposing sides of a case do in fact hate each other, because they have convinced themselves that they genuinely feel the passions they pretend or because they're inherently odious. More often, however, their passions are totally contrived. Below are seven of the most common litigation poses which you'll see used.

Righteous Indignation

Lawyers adopt this pose to suggest that their opponent's case is not only wrong in law but also ethically questionable. They use it when there is no law on their side.

Moral Outrage

This is like righteous indignation, only stronger. It is the pose of the divorce lawyer defending a self-made tycoon who has just abandoned his 50-year old wife for his 23-year old secretary and doesn't see why he should have to give up any of his hard-earned millions to support his first wife.

Disdain

This pose is adopted by lawyers defending one wealthy company against another. The aim is to convince the court that the plaintiff is just trying it on against your client, who obviously didn't *mean* to pour toxic waste into the kindergarten water supply.

Intimacy

This is the pose of hotshot London barristers trying to squash obscure plaintiffs represented by even more obscure juniors from the provinces. They use this pose, augmented by winks and hints of levity, to establish a personal relationship with the judge, suggesting without stating that *good* lawyers ("like you and me, Your Honour") can see that the plaintiff is a few sandwiches short of a picnic.

Bewilderment

This is the pose of the lawyer whose opponents have just scored a direct hit, and who have hammered home an argument to which he has no reply. He adopts a pose of utter bewilderment as a last-ditch effort to suggest that the argument makes little sense and is irrelevant to the facts of the case.

Sincerity

This "would-I-lie-to-you?" pose is used by defence lawyers attempting to counter popular assumptions about the culpability of certain categories of defendant. Battling against a jury which has already made up its mind, they adopt a pose that says "I *know* what it looks like, but believe me, Sir Henry was actually trying to get the girl *out* of his car." Occasionally, the jury is stupid enough to fall for the act.

Disappointment

With this pose a lawyer attempts to suggest that the devastating points just scored by his opponent are, to his sadness, underhanded and deceitful. Often the lawyer will season this pose with a pinch of parental solicitude, as if for a child gone astray.

*"Terrible day in Court, dear. I showed **disdain** when I meant to show **disappointment**."*

YOU AND "THE COURT"

Ten Commandments of Courtroom Conduct

➤ The judge is always "Your Honour" or "The Court".

➤ The judge's clerk is always "Your Honour" or "The Court".

➤ The judge is never "late", but sometimes "the press of business" interrupts her schedule.

➤ The judge's prior ruling is never "mistaken", but a contrary ruling may well be justified by "subsequent developments in the law".

➤ The judge is always to be thanked for her thoughtful ruling, even if she has just insulted you personally and made an exemplary damages award of £1 million against your client.

➤ The judge has never "forgotten" anything, but frequently you must "refresh the court's recollection" of key facts.

➤ The judge has never "neglected to read the court papers" but frequently you must "draw the court's attention" to key facts therein.

➤ The judge knows every relevant statute and case, so it is of course appropriate to introduce points of law with "As the court knows . . ."

➤ The judge will never "hold on" or "wait a second", but sometimes you may "beg the court's pardon" or "pray for the court's momentary indulgence."

➤ The judge never has to "visit the Ladies", but often "the court will take a brief recess."

CHAPTER SIXTEEN

LEGAL ETHICS

(And other Great Oxymorons)

The very concept of legal ethics triggers spontaneous laughter within the general populace. It is viewed as a monumental contradiction in terms. And yet lawyers profess to take legal ethics very seriously. It is a required part of the professional training, and receives lip service from judges, law professors, and professional organisations. For this reason if no other, and notwithstanding its irrelevance to current legal practice, every lawyer should at least have a passing familiarity with the Guide to the Professional Conduct of Solicitors.

The Guide contains rules governing virtually every aspect of practice set down in typical lawyerly form – that is to say, lengthy and unintelligible to laymen. It ranks up there with Kant's *Groundwork of the Metaphysics of Morals* as a cure for insomnia.

Part of the Guide is taken up with safety-net rules which have to be there just in case. Rule 7.01 is the ultimate regulatory catch-all ⟡

"A solicitor shall not do anything which might compromise or impair the good reputation of the solicitor's profession."

Of course. Grass is green, the sky is blue, and vomit is disgusting.

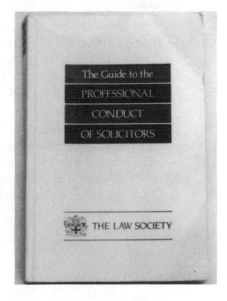

The Guide to the
PROFESSIONAL
CONDUCT
OF SOLICITORS

THE LAW SOCIETY

HOW FAR CAN YOU GO?

How far can you go in fulfilling your ethical obligation to represent your client diligently? Suppose your client is charged with stabbing someone in a dark alley. Can you ethically contend – indeed are you ethically *required* to contend – that he didn't actually stab the victim, but just happened to be holding the filleting knife when the victim walked into it . . . backwards . . . twenty-three times? Over the years, four tests have been developed for measuring which arguments are acceptable and which go too far:

➤ *The Smell Test.*

The most stringent of the four standards, this one precludes you from making any argument that just doesn't smell right. Lots of arguments smell so bad that people in court will be checking the soles of their shoes.

➤ *The Blush Test.*

If you can make a given argument without turning visibly red, it passes. The stringency of this test, like that of the two below, varies according to the shamelessness of the lawyer. In some firms it is entirely redundant.

➤ *The Gag Test.*

If you can utter a theory or alibi without upchucking from the outrageousness of your words, it passes. Known colloquially as the 'Amnesia at the Check-Out' Test.

➤ *The Wrath of God Test.*

This is an extremely liberal test, precluding only those arguments so insupportable that their very utterance is likely to cause lightning to strike you down even as you speak. This test is usually reserved for *extremely rich* clients with a lot to lose.

Other rules simply wouldn't need stating if Rule 7.01 had any effect:

"A solicitor shall not take unfair advantage of a client by over-charging for work done" and shall not act *"solely to gratify a client's malice or vindictiveness."*

But lawyers are prone to the same temptations as professionals supposedly a lot lower down the ladder of trustworthiness. They need constant reminding of even the most basic ethical tenets:

"To give an estimate that has been pitched at an unrealistically low level solely to attract the work, and subsequently to charge a higher fee is improper."

Of course, with architects you at least *know* when you're being ripped off: even complete bozos figure things ain't right when they can count the stars through the gaps in their roof extension.

Anyone who would promulgate such rules clearly has incredible faith in the power of words – the sort of person who would put a "Do not Steal" sign under the wipers of his XJS when he parks it in Heathrow Long-Stay for a month.

"Thurgood always enjoyed playing Devil's Advocate."

COURTESY AMONG LAWYERS
"After you, Dogbreath"

Time was, lawyers were extremely polite to one another. Courtroom conduct was a model of civility, and the refined intercourse of adversaries in litigation reflected Western civilisation at its peak.

Except for the courtesies still accorded to the bench (the so-called 'bootlick' imperative) those gentle and genteel days appear to be behind us now, as tempers go unchecked and mouths unmuzzled. A casual eavesdropper of the courtroom in the nineties is likely to hear references to "dubious assertions" and "theories of uncertain origin". A cursory perusal of courtroom transcripts will almost certainly turn up charges of "unfounded allegations" and "erroneous assumptions".

With this kind of language already commonplace, can slurs such as "questionable good faith" and "tendentious mischaracterisation" be far behind?

Little wonder that ours is considered an X-rated profession.

CHAPTER SEVENTEEN

THE CREATIVE ART
OF BILLING

*'Who says there are only
twenty-four hours in a day?'*

Anyone who thinks that lawyers lack imagination hasn't seen them fill out their time sheets.

If you hope to succeed in the law, it is essential to master the creative aspects of billing. As a trainee you can never tell your friends how you really spend your time; as an assistant, you can never tell partners how you really spend your time, and as a partner you can never tell clients what they're really being billed for.

Even if you're a lay person, it is important to understand the billing process. You'll still end up in hock to your lawyer, but at least you'll know where the money went.

The two time-sheets on the pages that follow illustrate the legal mind at its creative best:

The Cost of Going to Law

The Sunday Times reported that Lonrho's epic battle with Mohammed Al Fayed cost it more than £40 million in legal fees. Harrods spent a comparatively frugal £10 million.

When the rapprochement finally happened, Tiny Rowland wasted no time: "We were paying our QC £100,000 a month on retainer, plus VAT. That was just one man. As soon as I did the deal with Mohammed I telephoned Royston Webb, our legal director, and told him to turn off the taps."

WHAT THE TIME-SHEET *SAYS*

CLIENT: Global Magazines plc

Reviewing active client litigation files	2 hours, 5 minutes
Phone conference with client re same	1 hour

CLIENT: Sarawak Oil Inc.

Lunch conference with client on outstanding matters, including action being brought by native sheep farmers for environmental damage	2 hours, 20 minutes

CLIENT: Ryan Leg Growth Spa

Reviewing, editing and revising modified documents	3 hours, 55 minutes
TOTAL BILLABLE TIME	9 hours, 20 minutes

WHAT THE TIME SHEET *SHOULD* SAY

CLIENT: Global Magazines plc

Thinking about client's new receptionist during morning jog	30 minutes
Reading morning paper	25 minutes
Rummaging through client files for name and number of client's new receptionis	30 minutes
Getting coffee	15 minutes
Geting psyched up to call client's new receptionist re dinner on Saturday night, inlcuding preparing note to assist re same	1 hour, 15 minutes
Calling client's new receptionist re dinner on Saturday night	10 minutes

CLIENT: Sarawak Oil Inc.

Three-bottle lunch with client at Langan's

•Discussing client's golf game and recent holiday in St. Lucia	1 hour, 45 minutes
•Swapping ethnic jokes about sheep farmers	30 minutes

CLIENT: Ryan Leg Growth Spa

Proofreading retyped Agreement	1 hour, 20 minutes
Sleeping at desk	20 minutes
Proofreading re-retyped Agreement	1 hour, 20 minutes
Flirting with articled clerk	25 minutes
Arranging for copying of re-re-retyped Agreement	40 minutes
TOTAL BILLABLE TIME	9 hours, 20 minutes

"Aeroplanes and time zones are marvels of mankind.
They enable me to bill 25 hours in a day."

Multiple Billing

Perhaps the most ingenious device known to the law was conceived in response to the popular misconception that there are only twenty-four hours in a day.

Double-billing, or billing two clients for the same increment of time, occurs most frequently when a lawyer is required to travel. A lawyer based in Leeds who is required to visit London to confer with two clients might bill the four hour return train trip to each. His rationale is that if he had made the trip for one client alone, he'd have billed that client for all the time – so why not bill all of it to each?

Some lawyers double bill as a matter of course. None of them, especially not the ones who triple and quadruple bill, acknowledge that it goes on. They're greedy, not stupid. What they do is bury the double-billed time in the mountain of other items billed to the client, and no one is any the wiser.

The only way clients could monitor this practice would be to have access to what other clients were being billed by the same partner at the same time. They can't do that of course. Confidentiality laws require that lawyers keep their clients' affairs secret.

Confidentiality laws arose about the same time as double-billing.

CHAPTER EIGHTEEN

LAWYERS IN LOVE

'Dealing with Romantic Feelings towards a Lawyer'

You've heard the stories. Everyone has. They're not pretty. Maybe it's happened to someone you know. A friend or colleague. Maybe to someone you love – that's when it really hurts.

What on earth could possess someone to become romantically involved with a lawyer? To anybody who knows the profession, the idea is about as inviting as falling in love with an old jockstrap. An Italian unicyclist's jockstrap, even.

A prominent sociologist has compared the phenomenon of going out with a lawyer to the Cabbage Patch Doll craze that swept the world about fifteen years ago, except of course for the tragic consequences. And the fact that playing with Cabbage Patch Dolls offers the possibility of sexual gratification. Also, if you go out for dinner, you'll be more popular if you bring a Cabbage Patch Doll. And it's more likely to pick up the bill.

In fact going out with a lawyer isn't much like going out with a Cabbage Patch Doll at all. Still, some people continue to do it – go out with lawyers, that is.

What is to be done? Sadly, for those already involved, precious little *can* be done. Anyone who has fallen in love with a lawyer is beyond help. The only real hope lies in prevention. This can best be ensured by having nothing at all to do with lawyers except when it's absolutely necessary, like when you're about to hauled off to jail. Even then you might want to think about it . . . you know, taste the food, have a chat with your cell mate, give it a chance.

For most people, avoiding lawyers comes as naturally as breathing or, perhaps more appropriately, stepping on a cockroach. You see a lawyer and think, there but for the grace of God go I. You feel the same mixture of pity and revulsion you feel for a drunk in the gutter, except the drunk might be pleasant company.

As difficult as it may be for most people to conceive of falling in love with a lawyer, a few seem to do it every year. What kind of perverse love are we talking about? It's difficult to describe, but if you've ever talked to a sailor who's been away at sea for ten or twelve months, you have an idea of the desperation involved. It's similar to the craving that pupils at single-sex boarding schools experience towards the end of term, and which the Governors relieve by bussing in the 1st XV of the nearest boy's school.

Consider the case of Jennifer X. ("X" is not her real name) We'll call her Jennifer. She was an attractive young woman living in Fulham, SW6. She didn't get asked out very often, though. This is because she really wasn't that attractive. (More than a few people who met her later commented "I didn't know Wade Dooley was a transvestite") She wasn't all that young, either. But she did live in Fulham.

Jennifer was an unemployed former stockbroker in the City. The economic turmoil of the late eighties had cost many stockbrokers their jobs. Jennifer was made redundant a little while before the turmoil began, admittedly, but that's another story. Inevitably, she had lots of time on her hands, which she used not only to indulge her fondness for Belgian chocolates, but also to hang round the White Horse on Friday nights in the hope of meeting Mr. Right.

Enter Andrew Greenly – his real name; so what if a lawyer is publicly humiliated? He was a conscientious if modestly talented assistant at a large corporate firm in the City, and equipped with about the same social appeal as Jennifer.

Andrew and Jennifer first met on a Club Med holiday in Tunisia. They were both fighting for space at the hors d'oeuvre table, hurling food of every sort in the general direction of their heads.

Divorce Lawyers
Don Juans of the Profession

Relationships between lawyers and clients are fairly rare, except in the case of divorce lawyers when they are fairly common. Nothing wrong with that, you might say – divorce lawyers are entitled to a bit of nookie just as much as the rest of us.

The problem is that people going through the trauma of a divorce are often emotionally vulnerable. Is it fair for a randy divorce lawyer to take advantage of his position and his client's vulnerability to pursue his own sexual needs? A leading family judge thinks not. He believes it amounts to sexual exploitation and has called for the Law Society to introduce a code of practice to stop it.

Until that happens, the antics of one Midlands solicitor will no doubt continue unabated. He keeps a box of Kleenex in one desk drawer and a bottle of wine in the other – a tactic as unsubtle as it is successful. He claims twenty home runs in the last two years.

*"I am, among other things, a leading authority
on the laws of sewers and drains."*

Perhaps by fate they simultaneously made a grab for the same hors d'oeuvre, the last one of those mini-sausages soaked in honey, and their hands touched. Although both were initially repulsed by the contact, their long-starved sexual appetites quickly took over, and they left hand in hand, which repulsed everyone else, but Andrew and Jennifer were past caring about that.

Infatuation turned to passion. They spent every night together for the next six weeks. So inflamed was Jennifer's ardour that she was even willing to overlook Andrew's insistence on wearing his suit to bed. "I think it's the braces" he would say. "They make me feel so masterful."

By the end of the month they were engaged.

Jennifer's enchantment soon turned to frustration. As time went on, Andrew began dragging himself home later and later. It reached the point when Jennifer wouldn't know whether he was coming home at all, and when he did, usually around midnight, he would fall straight asleep. (still wearing his suit, as mentioned)

For a while, Jennifer suspected that he was seeing another woman. Some of his sleep-talking sounded vaguely licentious – terms like "joinder of parties", "ejectment" and "post-trial briefs". As blind as love is, however, she was able to make a realistic assessment of the chances of another woman becoming interested in Andrew, and she put the thought out of her mind.

Abstinence wasn't the worst of Jennifer's problems with Andrew. They didn't seem to communicate any more. Andrew had taken to addressing her in condescending tones, which she knew he had picked up from the way partners at the firm addressed him. Rather than simply talking with her, he seemed to be lecturing her, and he had the strange habit of summarising his argument at the outset and reserving three minutes for rebuttal.

Jennifer considered breaking off the engagement. All her friends said her goldfish was better company than Andrew, even though it had been floating at the top of the tank for a month. But it's a hard world for short, podgy, odd-looking, talentless former stockbrokers, and she decided to try to keep the marriage alive.

Only after she had had their first child, and realised how much it was going to be like Andrew – imagine a hairless rabbit in pinstripes – did Jennifer appreciate the full measure of her mistake.

Jennifer's story is a sad one, the story of a wasted life. But it need not be your story as well. Learn the lesson of her misfortune. The only way to handle romantic feelings towards a lawyer is not to have any.

Spotting Lawyers out on the Town

In a better world, lawyers would never set foot outside their offices. They'd just live there, eating, sleeping, billing. Some commercial firms have already attained this plateau. Many lawyers still wander the streets, however, and bumping into one can ruin an otherwise perfectly enjoyable Saturday evening. You're a friendly person. You enjoy meeting new people. But you have to draw the line somewhere.

Suppose you spot a lawyer near you in a pub. What do you do? Firstly, look around for others. They usually hunt in packs. Then spill a drink on his trousers. The prospect of losing the crease will have him running for his Corby press.

If a lawyer should take the clearly innappropriate step of initiating conversation with you, call the police and have him physically thrown out. Don't worry about hurting his feelings; he's used to this type of treatment. Some lawyers go out in public looking for abuse, craving that moment of self-discovery when their foreheads crunch against the pavement and their brogues get scuffed.

What if you're not sure whether the person in question *is* a lawyer? When you're seventeen pints into the evening, it may be hard to tell. The trouble is that you can't just come right out with it and ask him, because what if he's *not* a lawyer? Then, you've got a fight on your hands. Besides, what are the chances of anyone admitting to that kind of thing, especially when they're out in public trying to "pass"? Your best bet is to apply one of the following tests:

➤ Mention that your father is chairman of Glaxo, and that he is looking for a new solicitor. Then stare into his face. If his pupils dilate and saliva appears at the corner of his mouth, have him thrown out.

➤ Assert that legal fees should be subject to review by a panel of lay people. If the vein in his forehead starts to throb, have him thrown out.

➤ Declare that you've long considered expanding briefcases and dictaphones to be emblematic of a truly advanced society. If he nods in agreement, have him thrown out.

➤ Mention your admiration for people who know how to put the Inland Revenue in its place. If he smiles, puffs out his chest, and launches into a discussion of tax shelters and generation-skipping trusts, have him thrown out. (You may catch an accountant or two with this trick – no loss.)

If, despite all efforts, a lawyer causes irreparable harm to your night out, don't get mad. Get even!

Firstly, ask him for his business card. Take two or three. You never know when you'll back into someone else's car trying to get out of a tight parking space, and want to leave a note under the wipers.

Secondly, tell him that just a moment ago – what an amazing coincidence! – you were talking to someone who wants to hire a lawyer. And then give him the number of that old school friend who's been trying to sell you a pensions policy for the last six months.

Can you find the lawyer in this picture?

Model Contract for Lawyer going on a date

CONTRACT

Courtenay Bigguns-Lately (the "Dater")

and

Sally Forth (the "Datee")

1. Notwithstanding The Bill being a bit of a cliffhanger, or a last-minute pick-up at the Stoat & Fox after work, the Dater and the Datee agree to meet at *Chez Pierre's* at 8.30 p.m. on Friday (hereinafter referred to as the Date) always allowing that the Datee may be no more than 20 (twenty) and no less than 10 (ten) minutes late without incurring penalties under Rider 17(i): Emotional Blackmail.

2. It is hereby understood that the Date shall take place in order that the Dater may discuss a couple of really quite interesting ideas he's got for the litigation meeting on Tuesday on which he'd like some creative input from the Datee. Both parties shall terminate such discussion no later than 3 (three) minutes after the stuffed mushrooms have been served, at which point they shall undertake to determine from each other:

(i) Whether the Dater is still seeing Susan from Accounts (hereinafter referred to as "A Bit Tarty If You Ask Me, But Then Some Men Go For The Obvious Type");

(ii) Whether the Datee really stung that fool Nigel in Commercial for a five-course meal at Quaglinos plus entrance to Tramp;

(iii) How the Dater recalls the very first time he saw the Datee across the boardroom during another litigation meeting and even though they didn't speak until the Christmas Eve party, he'd always sort of thought, well, you know, she wasn't like the other girls, she was more, like, sensitive.

3. It is hereby agreed that at no time during the period of this contract shall the Datee draw attention to the following:

(i) the Dater's choice of the second cheapest bottle of wine

(ii) the Dater's belief that it is only a matter of time before Chris Rea makes it big again

(iii) the Datee's total lack of interest in whether the Quins should have played Carling, despite his injury, that afternoon, whoever Carling is, or, come to that, the Quins;

4. In consideration for this and notwithstanding that everybody knows who Carling is, boyish beefcake, plays inside centre, eats Quorn, the Dater agrees

(i) Not to eat all the after-dinner mints that come with the bill;

(ii) Not to cause embarrassment by paying with any credit card that causes the waiter to ask the Dater whether he would mind stepping over to the till for a second, thus making it clear to everybody in the restaurant that the Dater can't even run to a pizza, let alone and *inter alia* a good bottle of wine.

5. At the termination of the meal, the Dater agrees to conduct the Datee to her place of residence, *always notwithstanding* that should the Datee insist on traveling the six miles home alone, on foot, through a derelict housing estate and a freight marshalling yard, the Dater shall take this as fair notice to quit.

6. Always provided that the Datee does not leave the Dater standing on the doorstep (ref. That Fool Nigel, passim) the Datee agrees within 5 (five) minutes of crossing the threshold, to make it plain, by word or by deed, whether she is any of the following

(i) Not That Sort of Girl on a first date;

(ii) Not That Sort of Girl after a dodgy meal and a bottle of House Red;

(iii) Entirely That Sort of Girl, but not with the Dater.

7. Should Clauses 1 to 6 above be satisfied it is hereintofore agreed that neither party shall cause the following to be uttered:

(i) I don't do this with everyone I go out with, you know.

(ii) I'd like to stay, honestly, but I've got football training first thing. Now where's my other sock?

(iii) You won't tell anyone in the office about this, will you?

(iv) Damn! Look, er, I'm terribly sorry, I've never had this problem before.

(vi) Funny, that's not what Susan in Accounts says.

*" I find it helps to remember that the client is the one in trouble.
Nobody's talking about sending me to jail."*

CHAPTER NINETEEN

YOU AND YOUR LAWYER

'Finding him, Using him, Keeping him in his Place'

Sooner or later it happens to us all. Your life is going fine, you're keeping up with your mortgage payments, you've just been promoted, your sex life is finally heating up, and then, out of the blue, disaster strikes. Your playful Great Dane, good old Chewy, dismembers a small child; you have a few too many beers and on the way home decide to chance a red light, only to notice too late the local Chief Constable's elderly mother stepping off the pavement; your wife finds some pink lace underwear in your glove compartment and doesn't buy your story about how much more comfortable you find them than boxer shorts.

Law books are full of such tales of disaster. What makes them disasters is that when they happen you have to consult a lawyer.

You've hoped against hope that you'd never have to do it. You've never felt comfortable around lawyers. You've never associated them with the good things in life. But now there's no choice. Like appendicitis, your legal problem won't just go away. You have to *do* something about it and you can't do it on your own.

The analogy to appendicitis is instructive: getting rid of a legal problem, like having an organ removed, is painful, costly (your lawyer will perform a Walletectomy on you), and will leave you scarred for life. But since it has to be done, you want it done properly. You don't want to go down for five years for whistling *Colonel Bogie* in Burlington Arcade.

Selecting Your Lawyer

How do you go about the critical task of finding a lawyer? Just let your fingers jog through the Yellow Pages? Stroll down the high street and pick the first frosted glass window-front?

One of the difficult things about instructing a lawyer is that you don't necessarily get what you pay for. If you go to a big name firm you'll pay a fortune for the privilege, but the advice and the service you receive may be no better, and possibly even worse, than that available in the High Street at a fraction of the cost. This is particularly so if your case is relatively small as far as the big firm is concerned. Your lawyer will always have more important files to work on, and he'll probably hand your matter to his trainee as suitable material on which to cut his teeth. And make mistakes.

The other truism is that, although a *firm* may have an excellent all-round reputation, you as a client will be relying on an *individual's* ability and experience, not the firm's.

Clients tend to assume that lawyers at the top firms are all roughly as competent as each other. This is untrue. Law firms are a bit like racing stables: the stable that produced Red Rum trained lots of other nags whose career high point consisted of the top shelf at Tescos.

There's the same uneven distribution of talent in a law firm. The lawyer in charge of your case may only be on the payroll because his name bears a striking resemblance to the one at the head of the firm's notepaper, in which case all the expertise in other quarters of the firm will be totally irrelevant to your position.

At least as important as the question of *which firm*, then, is the question of *which individual*.

Go by Recommendation

A recommendation is your best bet. Ask your family, friends, or business colleagues if they can recommend someone. Don't expect glowing praise for any lawyer. No one has anything really good to say about them. Work to a lower benchmark, so that if someone describes Lawyer X as "a miserable old sod who hardly ever returns your calls" you recognise it for the high praise it is.

Shop Around

Set up appointments with five or six lawyers – as many as you can stomach. Remember that although the one you eventually instruct will probably bill you for the precious time you squandered in that first interview, the several who you don't will have to absorb the loss. (If one of them bills you for £100, feel free to use the invoice for cat litter. It'll never be worth his while to sue.)

When you arrive for your appointment, remember that you're master and he's slave, whatever it feels like. Some lawyers find the prospect of dealing with clients so abhorrent that they'll hold a scented hankie to their nose throughout your meeting. If your lawyer turns out to be one of those, remember that there are dozens of other firms you can turn to. Console yourself with the thought that no matter how bad things are, at least *you're* not a lawyer.

Ask the receptionist to let your lawyer know you've arrived. You will then be kept waiting for between fifteen minutes and an hour. It's irritating but inevitable. Just be grateful that you don't have to stand in a queue.

Waiting rooms will vary from firm to firm. Some are so grubby and down-at-heel, you will begin to feel that your problem isn't so bad after all. Others are innappropriately and disgustingly opulent. As you sit there waiting to be called, savour the luxury of filthy but thoughtfully-spent lucre: the marble floors, the mahogany-panelled lift, the exotic plants. Try not to think about who's paying for them.

Stay Cool

Eventually a secretary will arrive to escort you to the inner sanctum, where you will finally cast your eyes on the curiosity that may become your lawyer. Keep your wits about you at this stage. Take note of various points of manner, like whether he steps forward to shake your hand, or does so from behind his desk; whether he asks his secretary to hold any calls, or subjects you to interruptions from his other clients and/or partners and/or friends. These minor elements of behaviour are a reliable indication of the kind of service you can expect in the future.

Above all, do not be intimidated by him. Ask him what kind of success he's had in recent cases; ask him for the names of some recent clients who you can contact for a reference. Make him explain the difference between herringbone and tweed. Remember, he's not your lawyer yet.

DOCTORS v LAWYERS

Doctors and lawyers are notoriously unfriendly to each other. This seems strange at first, because they're all from the same sort of background, they live in the same streets, they're flip sides of the same professional coin.

Nevertheless, they don't like each other. What eats lawyers is the superior respect enjoyed by the medical profession. Doctors get special parking permits, allowing them to park in places normally reserved for people with no legs. Doctors get to be called 'Doctor', whereas lawyers are plain 'Mr'. Someone who comes bottom of his class at medical school is still called Doctor, whereas someone at the bottom of his class at law school is called waiter.

And whereas doctors are credited with performing a skillfull and valuable social service, lawyers are regarded as bloated leeches feeding on society's misfortunes.

Finally, whereas medical school is still very difficult to get into, practically anybody can get into law school somewhere. Just think about the lawyers you've met. Some are bright enough, but how many will be picking up prizes in Stockholm?

Discuss the Fee

One matter you should always raise in your initial meeting is the question of fees. Although under an obligation to provide estimates if asked for them, lawyers aren't always so eager to bring the subject up on their own.

Even when you ask directly, they can be strangely cryptic in response, as if the subject is too crass for discussion. Don't be taken in by this pose and reject evasive answers. You don't want to discover too late that your lawyer's casual reference to "my usual rate" means £300 per hour. Neither should you settle for "Oh, I think we can work something out that will be mutually satisfactory." Hey, if you weren't desperate, you wouldn't be paying him anything.

Be prepared to have to work for an answer. He might attempt full-scale diversionary tactics, as in:

"That's a good question, Ms Stephenson, and I'm glad you had the presence of mind to raise it at the outset. Too often, I think, lawyers are so busy striving to advance their clients' interests that they lose sight of these kinds of questions and neglect to establish any true understanding – or what could be called a meeting of minds – as to how it will all turn out in the long run. Why, I recall one case I had down in Bristol ....."

When this romp through irrelevance finishes, repeat the question. Do so again and again until you get a straight answer or the cleaning people come in to vacuum and turn off the lights.

As a general rule law firms are a lot more flexible on fees now than they used to be. This isn't an entirely voluntary conversion – it reflects the hard times firms have been through, and the growing savviness of clients. Competitive tendering, beauty parades, blended rates, discount billing and loss leading are pretty much the order of the day where big legal work is concerned. Firms do it because they have to do it.

But put things in perspective – City firms are still the most expensive in the world. According to 'International Financial Law Review 1000', City partners charge between £235 and £350 per hour. Hong Kong firms are the second most expensive at £235-£315 per hour. US firms are ostensibly cheaper with a maximum rate of £250 per hour, but they bill more hours per day by, for instance, charging for a lawyer's on-the-road breakfast and marking it up.

Only one thing will hold rates at bay, and that is competition. The growing numbers of American law firms in London will trim the sails of the home team and where Western firms have sought to operate outside the West – in Moscow for instance – they have had to match the much lower rates of local firms to get work.

You Call the Tune

The basic rule is: your lawyer works for you, not vice versa. You pay the piper, you call the tune.

Early on in the relationship you will find your lawyer telling you what you can and cannot do. Nip this in the bud. Tell him what *you* want, and if he can't make it happen, let him know you're prepared to take your business down the road. If he values your business at all (and lawyers

"Legal questions are never cut-and-dried, Mr Dodson. The fact that you're paying through the nose for our services doesn't mean we can guarantee results."

nowadays are having to be a lot less choosy about what they value and what they don't) you will be surprised at how quickly he will determine, after a little additional research, that what you want seems to be possible after all.

Monitor your Lawyer's Work

Every single thing that your lawyer does for you starts the meter running. It doesn't matter if he's just *thinking* about sending you a letter or

memo. If he's doing anything that so much as reminds him of you, you'll be billed for the time. What can you do to control this horrific scenario?

You have to play him at his own game by recording in painstaking detail exactly what benefits you're aware of receiving. Phone calls are a good place to start. Get in the habit of noting down the length of each call you have with your lawyer, when it occurred, what was said, and who initiated it. And don't be embarrassed to let him know you're doing just that, as in "Thanks for the call, John. I think we covered a lot in *just five minutes.*"

Every letter you write should make it clear that you are keeping an eagle eye on costs and don't intend to be shafted. There's nothing at all wrong in saying, "I enclose the information you requested. *In order to minimise the work your firm will have to do on the case, and hence minimise your costs,* I have filed the documents in chronological order, and high-lighted the important points."

It might aggravate him a little, and he won't like you for it, but when he comes to fill in that all-important time sheet, he'll err on the side of caution.

If, on the other hand, he gets the idea that you're not too worried about the size of your bill, it will expand in ways you cannot imagine. It will take on expensive dinners, exotic travel, and his wife's subscription to Vogue, not to mention peripheral research that would have been done anyway for other clients – things that ICI may not mind subsidising, but you do.

Keep your Perspective

Remember that your lawyer is, at the end of the day, only a lawyer. That you go to him to solve a problem, and that you tell him things you would not tell your doctor, best friend or spouse, does not alter the fact that his interest in you is purely commercial. He might sound as if he's interested in the details of your botched hip operation. You might appreciate his expression of outrage as you describe your wife's infidelities or your husband's violent tendencies when he reaches his sixth scotch of the evening. But remember that each word you utter, your lawyer's meter is clicking away. If that meter isn't running, your lawyer isn't listening.

CHAPTER TWENTY

LEGAL GLOSSARY

Of Foreign and Forked Tongues

Accord and Satisfaction

• The resolution of a claim for breach of contract, whereby the parties agree to alter the original terms.

• Carnal activity in the back seat of a Honda.

Action

• Law suit. A term used by lawyers to distract the client from the fact that absolutely nothing is happening on his case.

Adultery

• The crime of having more fun than society considers it seemly for an adult to have.

Affidavit

• A client's sworn statement of whatever facts his lawyer considers are essential to win the case.

A Fortiori

• "For a still stronger reason". A Latin term used by lawyers to link an unarguable premise to a bizarre conclusion.

Allegation

• A factual statement pertaining to proceedings. (See allegory, fable)

Amicus Curiae

• *Latin*, "Friend of the Curious". The person who works on the Enquiry Desk at the Royal Courts of Justice.

Arbitrator

• An independent negotiator. Derived from a combination of *arbitrary* and *traitor*.

Arguendo

• *Latin*, "For the sake of argument", or

'hypothetically speaking'. Not to be confused with *innuendo* – a popular Italian suppository.

Bankruptcy

• Life after debt.

Brief

• A legal term which, to the extent that it suggests brevity, constitutes the only one-word oxymoron in the English language.

Briefcase

• A leather lunch box.

Capital Gains Tax

• Accrual and unusual punishment.

Contributory Negligence

• In London, the doctrine that anyone who leaves their car guarded by any-thing less than a regiment of Greenjackets is as much to blame as the person who stole it.

Damnun Absque Injuria

• *Latin*, "Loss without Injury". A polite reference to the retirement of non-productive senior partners. (See Rule against Perpetuities)

Deadwood

• Anyone in your firm who is senior to you.

Dictaphone

• A battery-powered device beloved by lawyers for its inability to fall asleep during legal monologues.

Euthanasia

• A system of early retirement often urged on highly paid senior lawyers by their younger partners.

Ex Lax

• *Latin*, "From the Lawyer". Refers to memos, briefs and other product of lawyers.

Fee Tail

• A restricted form of property ownership. Not to be confused with "Free Tail" (see Club 18-30)

Force Majeure

• An irresistible force that prevents you from fulfilling your contractual obligations – such as a storm, flood, war, or the realisation that you could make a much bigger profit elsewhere.

Habeas Corpus

• *Latin*, "Have you got a body!" A chat-up line used at legal conventions.

Hung Jury

• A divided jury. Ironic term, because if the jury's hung, the defendant isn't.

Layman

• What lawyers call the person they screw.

Legal Pad

• The residence of a cool lawyer.

• That extra something built into a lawyer's bill.

Litigation

• A basic right of the legal system, which guarantees every aggrieved person his decade in court.

Nuisance

• Wrongful interference with

someone's enjoyment of his property e.g. your thoughtless neighbour upstairs who insists on playing loud rock music at times when decent people like you are trying to sleep – not to mention the ill-bred insomniac downstairs who has taken to banging on his ceiling with a broom handle just because he can't appreciate the tasteful melodies (and other rhythmic sounds) that emanate from your flat at various reasonable times.

Objection

• The strangulated cry of a lawyer who sees truth about to enter the courtroom.

Paralegal

• A legal secretary who can't type.

Parole

• A conditional release from prison, allowing the convict to demonstrate the inadequacy of the original sentence.

Rainmaker

• A lawyer whose compensation bears no relation to his legal skills.

Res Ipsa Loquitur

• *Latin*, "It won't stop talking." A legal defence to the of killing mothers-in-law.

Settlement

• A device by which lawyers obtain fees without working for them.

Tax Lawyer

• Someone with a flair for numbers but without the personality to be an accountant.

Usufruct

• In real property law, the right to enjoy the fruits of land owned by someone else.

• An Italian gesture of contempt.

Vagina

• Aren't you a little old to be looking up words like this ?

Will

• A device which lets you wait until you're out of harm's way before revealing how you really feel about your spouse and children.

OTHER HARRIMAN HOUSE BOOKS

Title	Order Ref	Price*
• **'The Official High-Flier's Handbook'** ('How to Succeed in Business without an MBA') by Philip Jenks and Jim Fisk, paperback	HF	£8.99
• **'The Official Doctor/PatientHandbook** ('A Consumer's Guide to the Medical Profession') by Dr John Duckworth, paperback	ODH	£8.99
• **'Goldenballs'** (A gripping account of the legal battle between Sir James Goldsmith and Private Eye by Richard Ingrams), hardback	GOLD	£9.99
• **The Official Lawyer's Handbook** (Who knows? You may want to give extra copies to your frlends, colleagues, lawyer, . . . cell mate. Geat books don't last for ever. Get some stock in now!)	OLH	£9.99

*Prices include
£1 for p&p

ORDER FORM ON THE BACK PAGE OF THIS BOOK

FRAMED CARTOONS

NY *"So you went to law school, and now you want to practise law. I think that's sweet."*

PD *"The important thing in litigation is to have your Court documents prepared well in advance of the hearing."*

FL *"Can you find the lawyer in this picture?"*

Fifteen classic legal cartoons by artists including Ken Pyne, Johnny Pugh, Michael Goodman, and Martin Honeysett. Ideal for offices, halls, conference and reception rooms. They come smartly framed, with a bevel-cut double mount (cream outer, blue inner), in a black frame which measures 14" by 11.5".

Any 1: £32.00	≥9: £28.00 each

LM *"Let me get this straight . . . the perpetrator, a blonde Caucasian female, trespassed on your land, broke and entered into your dwelling, sat on your chairs, consumed your porridge, and slept in your beds. Is that right?"*

LQ *"Legal questions are never cut-and-dried Mr Dodson. The fact that you're paying through the nose for our services doesn't mean we can guarantee results."*

FRAMED CARTOONS

MM *"We practise law to make money. Fordham. If you can think of a more compelling reason . . . let's hear it."*

NG *"Nice guys, but an odd firm . . . they practise the law of the jungle."*

HR *"I tell you, Christine, it's the height of the art . . . a document composed entirely of fine print and disclaimers."*

RS *"Mather there is our rising star . . . billed 2400 hours last year, and has set his goals even higher for this year."*

AN *"And.naturally, there will be a search fee."*

HC *"Now you're in big trouble. Here comes my solicitor."*

FRAMED CARTOONS

MB   *"Looks like they mean business this time."*

BM   *"Be ever mindful, Farson, that not only must justice be done – it must be paid to be done."*

LS   *"Of course we had to consult our legal department first."*

AN   *"And naturally, there will be a search fee."*

COFFEE MUGS

THE COURT AWARDS MUG

The mug illustration (left) is from an 1890s magazine article and shows average court awards for different limb losses. The journalist revealed "a very handsome margin of profit" for successful plaintiffs, since damages far exceeded the costs of artificial limbs. A copy of the article comes with the mug.
CO Court Awards Mug £7.50

GUARANTEE
We guarantee every item fully to meet your expectations, or we will refund your money without question. Just return any purchase within 21 days.

I ♥ RICH CLIENTS MUG

The truth and nothing but the truth. A 10 oz white ceramic mug to enjoy your morning cuppa.
CM Rich Clients Mug £7.50

LAWYER T-SHIRTS

Sizes: M, L, XL

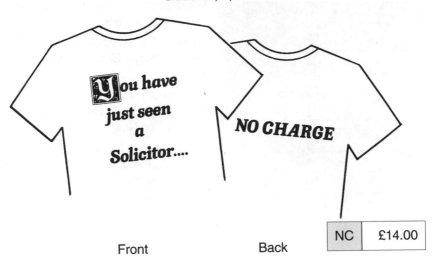

Front   Back

| NC | £14.00 |

(White with red and blue print, 100% quality Irish cotton)

T-Shirt
98% cotton, 2% poly

| TR | £14.00 |

Both in grey with blue motif

Sweat Shirt
70% cotton, 30% poly

| TRS | £25.00 |

Both in grey with blue motif

Legal Advice Dice

Solve problems instantly with the Legal Advice Dice.

• The first advises on strategy: Sue, Settle, Hedge, Beg, Ask Mum or Shoot.

• The second advises on tactical timing: Do, Don't, Soon, Later, A.S.A.P! or Now.

Indispensable for lawyers who are fed up with being asked for free legal advice, the dice come in a handy cotton pouch.

LF	£8.00

Sue The Bastards!

This venerable figure dates from the 1960s. Mothballed for twenty-five years, we kept on being asked by lawyers if we would bring him back, so we commissioned a new batch.

The statuette is seven inches high and hand-painted. We only have limited stocks, so if you want one don't hang around.

SD	£35.00

LITIGATION PAPERWEIGHT

This handsome paperweight depicts the best known legal cartoon of all – the 18th century parody of a lawsuit in which the plaintiff pulls one end of the cow, the defendant the other end, while the lawyer sitting between the two does the milking. *Plus ça change!*

The picture is in colour.

The paperweight is handcrafted in glass, measures 4" by 2.5" and comes in a smart gift box.

LG	£15.00

FOR JUNIOR LAWYERS

White terry cloth bibs in blue and red colours, to suit both boys and girls. Great gifts for a lawyer's child, or for just-made-up junior partners.

JP Junior Partner	£3.50
MQ Mess Ipsa	£3.50

LEGAL LOCKER ROOM

ORDER FORM

Ordered by	**Deliver to:** (complete only if different from left)
(MrMrs/Ms)	(MrMrs/Ms)
Name	Name
Address	Address
Postcode	Postcode
Daytime phone no.	Gift message:

Code	Product	Size	Price	Qty	Total

Sub Total	
ADD VAT*	
TOTAL	

PAYMENT METHOD

• **Cheque**
I enclose a cheque payable to 'Harriman House' for £

• **Credit Card**
Please debit my Visa/Access/Mastercard £

Card expiry date: end   /

Card Number:

Signed _____

*Currently 17.5% VAT for everything *except* books and the bibs (zero-rated)

For ultra-fast service PHONE your order on 01730 233870 or FAX it on 01730 233 880

Return this form (or a photocopy of it) to

    Harriman House, 7 The Spain,
    Petersfield,
    Hants, GU32 3JZ

• Delivery usually within 10 days, rarely longer than 21. • If your order is urgent, please write a deadline date on your order form. • A VAT invoice will be sent with your order. • If for any reason you are not satisfied with your products, return them to us for full refund.